DEATH KNELL

DEATH KNELL
by James Cawood

JOSEF WEINBERGER PLAYS

LONDON

DEATH KNELL
First published in 2017
by Josef Weinberger Ltd
12-14 Mortimer Street, London W1T 3JJ
www.josef-weinberger.com
plays@jwmail.co.uk

Copyright © 2017 by James Cawood
Copyright © 2016 by James Cawood as an unpublished dramatic composition

The author asserts his moral right to be identified as the author of the work.

ISBN: 978 0 85676 352 6

This play is protected by Copyright. According to Copyright Law, no public performance or reading of a protected play or part of that play may be given without prior authorization from Josef Weinberger Plays, as agent for the Copyright Owners.

From time to time it is necessary to restrict or even withdraw the rights of certain plays. It is therefore essential to check with us before making a commitment to produce a play.

NO PERFORMANCE MAY BE GIVEN WITHOUT A LICENCE

AMATEUR PRODUCTIONS
Royalties are due at least one calendar month prior to the first performance. A royalty quotation will be issued upon receipt of the following details:

Name of Licensee
Play Title
Place of Performance
Dates and Number of Performances
Audience Capacity and ticket price(s)

PROFESSIONAL PRODUCTIONS
All enquiries regarding professional rights should be addressed to Josef Weinberger Plays at the address above.

OVERSEAS PRODUCTIONS
Applications for productions overseas should be made to our local authorised agents. Further information can be found on our website or in our printed Catalogue of Plays.

CONDITIONS OF SALE
This book is sold subject to the condition that it shall not by way of trade or otherwise be re-sold, hired out, circulated or distributed without prior consent of the Publisher. **Reproduction of the text either in whole or part and by any means is strictly forbidden.**

Printed by Short Run Press Ltd, Exeter

To the memory of my father, John R Cawood

DEATH KNELL was first presented (under the title DEATH TOLL) by Talking Scarlet at the Theatre Royal, Windsor on 11th April 2016 prior to a national UK tour. The cast was as follows.

HENRY ROTH	George Telfer
EVELYN ROTH	Corrinne Wicks
JACK WILLOUGHBY	Anton Tweedale
DETECTIVE CHIEF INSPECTOR LAZAN	Jolyon Young

Directed by David Janson

Set design by Geoff Gilder

Lighting Designed by David North

CHARACTERS

HENRY ROTH

Mid-fifties. Walks with a stick.

EVELYN ROTH

His wife. Early thirties.

JACK WILLOUGHBY

Mid-twenties. Handsome and fresh-faced.

DETECTIVE CHIEF INSPECTOR LAZAN

Early forties.

ACT ONE

A renovated former shooting lodge that sits at the head of a loch in the Highlands of Scotland. Most probably Victorian, the house has been substantially altered and although far from being ultra modern it has all the comforts and amenities that suggest a large amount of money has been spent on the décor whilst maintaining its Highland charm.

We are in the entrance hall / living room of the lodge. Upstage centre and raised slightly on a step is the heavy wooden front door. On either side of this door are two large sash windows with window seats. The windows look out over a gravel driveway that gives way onto the rocks and eventually the loch. Upstage left is a door leading to the kitchen diner and ultimately outside. Centre stage left is a fireplace and mantelpiece. A basket of logs and a small pile of newspaper for kindling. Just below this is a mahogany desk with a cordless telephone and a laptop computer on top. The desk has a locked drawer within. A small window gives whoever sits at the desk a view out over the landscape. On the wall above the desk is a poster for a play entitled "Bloodlust". It is covered in four and five-star reviews. Centre stage we see a large comfortable settee and two matching armchairs. A large, low coffee table sits in the middle of the chairs. A script and a pen are placed on top of this table. Underneath the table is a large, heavy rug. Upstage right a staircase that leads to the first floor and the bedrooms. Downstage right another door leads to a library. This door is currently ajar. Next to this door is a small, well-stocked drinks table.

Although exuding grandeur and success, this is a cosy home, lived in and comfortable, which is perhaps at odds with its remote and lonesome situation. We are a good twenty-minute drive along a narrow valley road from the nearest town and the closest neighbours are sheep.

As the lights come up we can hear the lapping of the loch against the nearby rocks, the persistent & determined fall of Scottish rain and an occasional gust of wind.

7 p.m. on a cold and damp November evening. The fire crackles and spits against the chill in the air. The room is dark save for the light from the fire and a dull glow from the library doorway.

Then, emanating from unseen depths of the house (most probably the first floor landing) the hauntingly deep and sonorous toll of a grandfather clock marking the time.

We hear a car slowly pull into the driveway, its headlights ghosting briefly into the room. The car stops and the engine dies. A car door slams and footsteps are heard approaching, crunching on the gravel. The door begins to open.

Suddenly a blood-curdling scream is heard offstage.

The front door opens and EVELYN *enters. She is wearing a raincoat and holding a box of groceries. Because of the groceries she struggles to shut the door and has to use her foot to kick it closed behind her. She places the groceries on a window seat and takes her coat off, hanging it on a coat stand by the front door. She glances towards the library door.*

Another scream is heard, then a gunshot. EVELYN *just shakes her head before picking up the box again and walking into the kitchen.*

A beat later, HENRY *appears at the library door. He rests on his cane and sips from a tumbler of whisky.* EVELYN *re-enters from the kitchen, hits a light switch then jumps on seeing* HENRY.

EVELYN   Henry! For God's sake.

HENRY	Expecting someone else?
EVELYN	What are you doing, skulking in the shadows?
HENRY	Hardly skulking, just watching.
EVELYN	That's almost as bad.

(EVELYN *goes to stoke the fire and generally tidy up, taking a mug from the coffee table, tidying up the pages of script and rearranging cushions on the chairs.*)

HENRY	How do you do it?
EVELYN	Do what?
HENRY	Within seconds of coming home you make it seem as if a madman had ransacked the place.
EVELYN	Just tidying.
HENRY	Was it really that messy?
EVELYN	It's not personal. It's just tidying.
HENRY	Tidying, yes.

(EVELYN *notices something in the library with dismay.*)

EVELYN	You're just going to leave the TV on?

(*She enters the library and a moment later comes back in carrying a plate and a half empty family sized packet of crisps. She makes her way back towards the kitchen.*)

EVELYN	You know there's something deeply narcissistic about a playwright watching his own work over and over again.
	(*She exits into the kitchen.*)
HENRY	(*shouting after her*) I like to be reminded of my own genius.
EVELYN	(*off*) I rest my case.
	(HENRY *goes and pours himself another drink, the bottle runs out.*)
HENRY	Did you buy any more whisky?
EVELYN	(*reappearing with a fresh bottle*) I did.
HENRY	(*taking the bottle*) And how was that?
EVELYN	What a funny question.
HENRY	Not really.
EVELYN	Well it was hardly the most exciting part of my day.
HENRY	You know what I mean.
EVELYN	It was fine. Wasn't an issue.
HENRY	Well, that's progress.
EVELYN	I'm stronger than you think.
HENRY	No you're not.
EVELYN	Stop being so damned patronising, Henry. I am fine.

HENRY	Well, that's me told. I shan't care from now on.

(*Pause.* EVELYN *moves to break the moment.*)

EVELYN	Watching an adaptation of a play you wrote ten years ago seems a little . . .
HENRY	Yes . . . ?
EVELYN	Reflective.
HENRY	Reflective? Well, yes, I suppose it is. But nothing I have written since has come close to being as good.
EVELYN	Not this again.
HENRY	It's true. Sure, it's all produced, it's well received, the box office is acceptable . . . blah blah blah . . . but none of them are *hits*. I mean, real bloody *hits*. (*Indicating the poster.*) But that was. That was a smash, a wonderful, seismic smash. A year on the West End, eight months on Broadway, translated into twelve languages. That, my darling, is a hit. And I like to be reminded that I wrote one once. Rather than all the mundane rubbish I've produced since.
EVELYN	If you're fishing for compliments . . .
HENRY	I'm fishing for another hit. I couldn't care less about compliments. A year on the West End is a bloody compliment! Why do you think I watch the TV adaptation so often?
EVELYN	Because it's repeated all the bloody time.

HENRY	Because it's the only one of my plays that was deemed good enough to be adapted. It reminds me that I was once good enough for TV.
EVELYN	Then write for TV.
HENRY	Don't be ridiculous. No writer worth their salt actually wants to write for TV. They just want their stuff on it. From stage to screen. It's a yardstick, a measure that the public loves your work so much they want to see it in the comfort of their own home again and again.
EVELYN	(*almost to herself*) And again and again.
HENRY	(*but he isn't listening*) And all I've got is one lousy adaptation and a list the length of my arm of half-baked thrillers produced in Leatherhead, Leeds and Lichtenstein.
EVELYN	For God's sake! Henry, look around you. Look at the house you have, the ridiculous four-by-four I have just driven to the supermarket, the jewellery you buy me, the food we eat. Whatever else you've written may be *mundane* as you call it but they have made you rich and loved.
HENRY	*Loved?* Really?
EVELYN	You're just feeling sorry for yourself. You've had too much whisky and you're being morose.
HENRY	But now it's all going to change.
EVELYN	What is?

HENRY	Everything. You'll see. I'll be back. Back on top. No more mundane. No more *passable*. This . . . (*He holds up the script from the table.*) . . . is the new hit! Seismic. This script is seismic.
EVELYN	I do hope so, darling. For your sake.
HENRY	What does that mean?
EVELYN	Just that I want you to be happy.
HENRY	You do?
EVELYN	Of course.
HENRY	Well, then. Tonight is going to be good for both of us.
EVELYN	Tonight? Why?
HENRY	Well, that would be telling.
EVELYN	Please don't talk in riddles.
HENRY	We're having a guest.
EVELYN	But Henry . . . ! We said we weren't going to have any visitors. Not for a while, anyway. Not until I felt . . .
HENRY	But you said you're feeling stronger every day.
EVELYN	Yes, but still . . . oh, Henry, I have nothing prepared. I don't think I can play the hostess, not yet.
HENRY	You won't have to. He's here to see me, not you. I promise, all you'll have to do is say

	hello, smile graciously and sneak off. Unless you feel like you ought to stay for any reason.
EVELYN	And why would I want to do that?
HENRY	Oh I don't know, you may find him . . . intriguing.
EVELYN	Who is it? Do I know him?
HENRY	I don't see how you would. He's from my world. An actor.
EVELYN	Oh, not an actor. Here? You know what I'm like with all your actor friends. They're all so loud and brash and they drink so much. We moved up here to get away from all that.
HENRY	I think this chap is different. He's only just started and he's not had time to get like that. Still normal. That's why he's perfect.
EVELYN	Perfect? For what, exactly?
HENRY	For murdering.
	(*Pause.*)
EVELYN	I'm sorry?
HENRY	He's perfect for the fine art of premeditated death.
EVELYN	Well if you're not going to be serious . . .
HENRY	I'm being perfectly serious, I wouldn't joke about such things.

EVELYN	I don't understand. And now you've got that look.
HENRY	Look?
EVELYN	Your glazed look, like a dark cloud has passed behind your eyes.
HENRY	Poetic. Maybe you should be the writer.
EVELYN	I don't like it. It could be the whisky, I suppose . . .
HENRY	Could be.
EVELYN	But all this vague talk of murder . . .
HENRY	It's only vague because you don't know what's going on.
EVELYN	Then tell me. Who is this guest and why is he coming?
HENRY	Darling, there's no need to get so worked up . . .
EVELYN	. . . Because for a while now you've been like this. Talking in riddles and . . . watching me from all corners of the room.
HENRY	I've always enjoyed watching you.
EVELYN	And don't I know it.
HENRY	Because I love you. I like to watch you without you knowing.
EVELYN	Without me knowing? Really . . . you think I can't *feel* your eyes?

HENRY   I'm sorry if you don't like it.

EVELYN   It's not that. It's that you used to watch me . . . perhaps you used to watch me with love. In a way. But lately it's different.

HENRY   My eyes aren't what they used to be.

EVELYN   Don't try and be funny. Has something changed?

HENRY   That's a very, very complicated answer. We've been married for over five years, and five years can alter people, irreversibly. So yes, things may have changed. But I look at you in the same way I always have.

EVELYN   And how is that exactly?

(*Beat.*)

HENRY   I hope you don't mind me saying that this seems to be a gross overreaction to the somewhat commonplace news that we are to receive a guest this evening.

EVELYN   So tell me, for God's sake. Who is he?

HENRY   I've told you. An actor.

EVELYN   But why bring an actor all the way up here? Isn't it usual for you to meet them in London, audition them? Chat to their agent? Not invite them all the way up to the highlands of Scotland, ten hours away and entertain them at your own home.

HENRY   Granted, it's unusual. But then the situation that has presented itself is unusual.

EVELYN	How so?
HENRY	Because of this. (*He holds up the script.*) I finished it when you were at the clinic. I needed something to occupy my mind and I wrote like a man possessed. Not since "Bloodlust" have I written with such vigour and determination. And you see that's what thrillers need. When you're writing about base human emotions, pure anger, fury and of course, murder. You have to write with fire and speed and when you were away . . . well, I was energised. And within a matter of days I'd finished the first draft. Dare I say, the best first draft I've ever written. And I was sitting at that desk having just written the final line, about to email it to my agent, when I was struck by a thought. I was so pleased with it I didn't want to do it the disservice of simply sending it through the ether. So I decided there and then, to take it myself. In person.
EVELYN	To London?
HENRY	Exactly.
EVELYN	(*perhaps moving to a window*) Well . . . that's not so unusual, I suppose.
HENRY	I suppose not. We've lived up here for a year now. And I do love it. These desolate shores. It was always a dream of mine to live by a lake and here we are, not forty yards from one. Or is it a loch, now we're north of the border? But one does miss . . . what is it exactly? The noise and energy. After so many years in a big city, it's no surprise that here I was and suddenly everything seemed to be so quiet. Lonely. And I wanted to surround myself with the blanket of chaos

	that is London. I bet even you occasionally miss the big city.
EVELYN	I can't say I do.
HENRY	No? Well I found I did. So, I packed an overnight bag and took the train. Delivered the script, which, I hasten to add, was met with very positive responses and had a thoroughly lovely time. But there's a problem. A role in this play, the murderer in fact, requires a very specific type of actor. I don't want a star in the role; they'll ruin it with their ego. I want an unknown. Luckily my agent reminded me of the perfect young man. Not so long ago I was invited to Press Night for a new play. A dreadfully avant-garde piece about God-knows-what, but the critics fawned all over it. The cast were all strutting and huffing and being very clever and 'tormented' . . . all sweat and grimaces. Except one, one young man who was playing the smallest of parts. I don't even know if he had a line. Not one line. But he was so . . . honest. He was all my agent and I could talk about during the interval. So when we were discussing this role in my play, whom should we start talking about but this same young man. Oh Evelyn, you should see him. No awareness of his talent. And yet, there's a quiet confidence and a dark shadow across him . . . he's innocent and yet he could easily be a murderer. A madman. I wouldn't put it past him to be one of those charming sociopaths. You know the type. Gets you into bed and then cuts you up into small pieces.
EVELYN	Oh lovely, and you've invited him here?

HENRY	(*laughs*) I have! How exciting, don't you think? You see he may be perfect, but as we haven't started publicity or let anyone know about the play, it's all very hush-hush. No one can know. That's why I've invited him here. Away from London, away from casting directors and other playwrights who would suddenly swoop in and steal him from under my nose. That can't happen. This play needs him. I need him!
EVELYN	If I didn't know any better, I'd say you were in love with him.
HENRY	Jealous?
EVELYN	Of a penniless actor who could easily be a sex crazed sociopath? Dreadfully.
HENRY	Quite. So you see, darling, he's not here to see you. He's here to read the script, talk about the role and hopefully sign on the dotted line. You don't need to worry. Just be gracious.
EVELYN	I can at least be that.
HENRY	Good.
	(*He holds her face, almost threatening, and kisses her. She doesn't close her eyes.*)
EVELYN	So what's it called?
HENRY	Mm?
EVELYN	This new seismic hit. What's the title?
HENRY	"Death Knell".

EVELYN   "Death Knell"? Where did that come from?

HENRY   (*as he says this he walks behind* EVELYN *and holds her shoulders and almost wraps his hands around her neck, enjoying the drama*) From the depths of this very house. One evening, once you'd left, the light was dying in the valley and the shadows were creeping into the room like ink in water. A mist was gathering on the loch and there was no noise. I stopped typing and listened . . . straining to hear anything, any noise at all that would tell me that I wasn't totally alone on this earth. Then . . . amidst the encroaching darkness came the deep, echoed toll of the grandfather clock marking the hour. Marking the hour of the dead.

                (EVELYN *jumps and releases herself from* HENRY'S *grasp.*)

                Good title, don't you think?

EVELYN   I hate that clock. You know I do.

HENRY   It came with the house, Evelyn.

EVELYN   Well, I wish you'd get rid of it. Sell it. Smash it for firewood, I don't care. I just wish it would go.

HENRY   Smash it for firewood? No wonder "Antiques Roadshow" is lost on you. I think it has an atmosphere, adds a sinister air to the place. Perfect for murder.

EVELYN   Don't, Henry, please.

HENRY   Now come on, sit with me. He won't be here for a while yet. Sit.

(*She's about to sit . . .*)

Oh, did you buy the newspaper?

EVELYN   I did.

HENRY   Excellent.

EVELYN   (*knowing the answer*) Do you want me to get it?

HENRY   I think we've got time for an article or two, don't you?

(EVELYN *gets up and goes into the kitchen before reappearing with a newspaper.*)

And before I forget . . .

EVELYN   What?

HENRY   I gave you a little responsibility, didn't I? Before you went into town.

(*He stands up and puts out his hand.* EVELYN *goes over to her raincoat, produces a purse and takes out a bank card. She hands it back to* HENRY *who puts it in a pocket.*)

There we are. Well done.

EVELYN   I suppose you'll check the statement.

HENRY   Not unless I feel I have to.

(*Beat.*)

EVELYN   Henry . . .

HENRY   No. We've been through this.

EVELYN   I would like to go through it again.

HENRY   You will get the same answer.

EVELYN   (*throwing the newspaper down*) For God's sake!

HENRY   I don't know why you are so concerned about it.

EVELYN   I know I went into this marriage with my eyes wide open. Knowing what was expected of me. But surely, after five years. Five years . . . you can see why a woman of my age would like to be treated with the trust and respect owed to her.

HENRY   Trust?

EVELYN   All I am asking for is my own life. Outside of you. A life where I don't need you! Henry? Look at me.

                  (*He does.*)

                  My own money in my own bank account to do with as I please.

HENRY   And what would happen then? I put money into that account, because it sure as hell won't come from anywhere else. And one day I wake up and you've gone. Maybe you'll come back. But after what? After you've spent all the money on . . . (*Beat.*) I just don't want to find your body in a ditch or identify you in a morgue or God knows what else.

EVELYN   Please. You have to trust me one day. All the work I am putting in. All the time spent at the clinic. I won't have a drink. Not now. I promise.

HENRY All the time spent at the clinic?

EVELYN Yes.

HENRY Of course. (*Pause.*) I can't trust you, Evelyn. I can love you. But I can't trust you.

(*A tense moment between them.* EVELYN *may think about pursuing it further but realises it would be fruitless.*)

(*breaking the atmosphere*) Now come on. Read to me. My favourite part of the evening. Where I discover what's going on in the real world outside of this secluded glen.

(*He lies down on the settee.* EVELYN *sits on an armchair and searches the newspaper that she has picked back up.*)

EVELYN Any subject in particular? The Chairman of the Conservative Party has been forced to stand down amidst allegations of organising fetish sex parties at his home in Berkshire.

HENRY Kinky little bugger. That's public school for you. Next.

EVELYN (*finding something else*) Okay. Energy prices are expected to rise by nearly fifteen per cent due to . . .

HENRY Blah blah blah. I can afford it so I don't care.

EVELYN So said the concerned citizen.

HENRY	That's just the point, I'm not concerned. Give me news that will concern me. I want something *really* concerning.

(EVELYN *scans the pages.*)

EVELYN	(*suddenly struck by something*) Oh my God.
HENRY	What?
EVELYN	Listen to this. "Specialist Squad Brought In After "The Ghoul" – inverted commas – "Strikes Again."
HENRY	The Ghoul?
EVELYN	"A specialist murder squad from the Metropolitan Police has been called in following the discovery of a third body in rural Britain. Although the victim's identity is yet to be released, it is known to be the body of a thirty-three-year-old woman from South London. The body was found in an uninhabited holiday cottage in the remote Glen Rellik region of the highlands of Scotland." That's only down the road.
HENRY	Down the road? It's miles away. Carry on, don't stop . . .

(HENRY *is now sitting up and listening closely.*)

EVELYN	"This latest discovery follows those of two women of similar age who have been found within the last two months in the English Lake District and the Yorkshire Dales respectively. Police are convinced that it is the work of the same perpetrator and that the rural setting is some sort of

	'calling card'. All three bodies were found severely mutilated and with their throats cut. Commissioner Sir Geoffrey Brindle, of the Metropolitan Police today said "We are deeply concerned by recent events and are doing everything within our power to apprehend this criminal. This is why we are assisting all three local Police forces with the deployment of our specialist murder squad headed by Detective Chief Inspector Lazan of Scotland Yard. I can't stress enough . . ." And he goes on. God! How horrible.
HENRY	How exciting. A serial killer stalking the genteel Scottish countryside.
EVELYN	How can you say that? There are lives at stake. Our lives. He could be here. In this valley.
HENRY	Hardly. If they really thought that it wouldn't have been left to The Times to inform us. (*He gets up and goes to pour himself another drink.*) Look at the pattern. Lake District. Yorkshire. Here. It's a set route. These people, these psychopaths, they have all these things planned to the last detail. To their victims' very last breath.
EVELYN	Don't be so morbid.
HENRY	I'm just locking it away for a future reference.
EVELYN	Heartless.
HENRY	Professional.

(EVELYN *stands up and warms herself by the fire, stoking it. [At some opportune and natural moment during Act One the newspaper that has just been read from gets placed with the pile of kindling newspaper by the mantelpiece].*)

HENRY I'm sorry. You can't miss the irony though, can you?

EVELYN How do you mean?

HENRY When you think about it. Isn't that why we moved here? To get away from all of that.

EVELYN Is that really why we moved here? (*Pause.*) You know, you can't always keep me safe.

HENRY I can try.

(HENRY *takes up his script and reads.* EVELYN *studies him.*)

EVELYN London?

HENRY Mm?

EVELYN While I was away, you said you went to London to see your agent?

HENRY Yes, so?

EVELYN That's a ten-hour journey. (*Beat.*) And you didn't think to visit me?

HENRY What's that? (*He's now engrossed in his script.*)

EVELYN	Your agent's office is in Sloane Square. I was at the clinic on Cadogan Street.
HENRY	(*absentmindedly*) Mm.
EVELYN	Well, that's only a ten-minute walk. If that.
HENRY	Your knowledge of central London is very impressive my love, but where's this going?
EVELYN	Doesn't it strike you as odd that a husband whose wife is in a clinic only a few minutes from where he has a meeting doesn't do her the courtesy of paying her a visit?
HENRY	(*finding the thought almost distasteful*) Visiting? At the clinic? Hardly.
EVELYN	And why not?
HENRY	Well, it's not my place, is it? I didn't even know you were allowed visitors.
EVELYN	You never thought to ask.
HENRY	(*throwing script down*) No, to be quite honest, I didn't.
EVELYN	Or perhaps it's more to do with the fact that you're ashamed.
HENRY	Oh, for God's sake . . .
EVELYN	Well isn't it? Ashamed that your darling trophy wife is a spineless, weak-willed alcoholic locked away in a private rehab clinic.
HENRY	Do you really think that badly of me?

EVELYN	Well, what else am I meant to think? Out of sight out of mind, is it?
HENRY	That's as far from the truth as you can get.
EVELYN	Oh, really?
	(HENRY *moves out of frustration to the fireplace and stares into the flames.*)
	Or perhaps there's something else. Something you're not telling me.
	(HENRY *doesn't react, still staring into the fireplace.*)
	Another reason why you went to London.
HENRY	I told you, I went to see my agent. You can phone him and ask if you like.
EVELYN	I'm sure, but we all need a cover story occasionally.
HENRY	A suspicious mind is a dangerous one.
EVELYN	Then put my mind at rest.
	(*Pause.*)
HENRY	(*eventually turning to his wife*) I'm not a bad person, Evelyn. Whatever you may think. Whatever I may have done. I am not a bad man.
	(*A very strong gust of wind whips around the house and the rain lashes against the windows.*)

	(*shaking off the moment and moving*) He'll be swimming to the front door if he doesn't arrive soon.
EVELYN	How's he getting here?
HENRY	I gave him the details of the bus from town.
EVELYN	The valley bus?
HENRY	What other bus is there?
EVELYN	It's hardly reliable. I could have picked him up.
HENRY	The bus will be fine. He should be here any moment.
EVELYN	But he's still got quite a walk from the nearest stop.
HENRY	Has he? I wouldn't know, I never take it.
EVELYN	A fine way to welcome a guest.
HENRY	He's a fit young man. A bit of Scottish rain won't hurt him. (*Beat.*) Unless of course . . .
EVELYN	What?
HENRY	He's caught by The Ghoul!
	(*He switches the lights off by the wall for dramatic effect.*)
EVELYN	For God's sake, Henry! Turn the lights back on.
HENRY	What was that?

EVELYN Stop it!

HENRY No, honestly. I thought I saw something at the window.

EVELYN Henry! I'm being serious . . .

HENRY Oh my God!

EVELYN This is not funny!

(*Pause. Suddenly, a heavy banging on the door.* EVELYN *screams.*)

HENRY Bloody hell!

JACK (*off*) Hello? Hello . . . Mr Roth? Hello?

HENRY Oh, thank God for that.

(*He finds the lights and turns them back on again.*)

EVELYN Is that him?

HENRY Yes.

EVELYN I'm not ready.

HENRY Oh, for goodness sake. (*Shouting off.*) Just a second!

JACK (*off*) Oh . . . hello, Mr Roth. It's just me. Hope I'm not late.

HENRY No, no. Give me a second.

JACK (*off*) Yes, yes of course.

(EVELYN *has made her way to the window and is about to look out.*)

HENRY   Something wrong?

(*She stops.*)

If you're not ready, don't you think you should go upstairs?

EVELYN   Why?

HENRY   To freshen up. Change. You've been in those clothes all day.

EVELYN   You mean you want me to psyche myself up for a visitor.

HENRY   Have a little understanding.

(EVELYN *starts up the stairs but stops, turns around. Something's not right.*)

EVELYN   What did you say his name was again?

HENRY   I didn't. Now come on, it won't do to have the hostess absent.

(EVELYN *exits at top of stairs.*)

(*shouting off*) Just a second, young man!

(HENRY *makes his way to the desk, taking out his keys and unlocking a drawer. He takes out a brown A4 envelope, surreptitiously inspects the contents before throwing it down on top of the coffee table. He then goes to the door. Stops, prepares himself and takes a deep breath. Opens the door. We see* JACK, *pretty much soaked to the skin and cold.*)

HENRY   My dear boy, I am so sorry. Come in, come in.

JACK   Thank you, Mr Roth.

HENRY   Dear me, you're soaked. The highland rain is somewhat unforgiving. Let me take your coat.

JACK   Well, thanks.

(HENRY *helps him off with his jacket and hangs it on the coat stand.*)

HENRY   And let's put that down for the moment. You can take it up to your room later.

(HENRY *takes* JACK'S *small rucksack and places it on window seat.*)

You travel light. I wish my wife would take a leaf out of your book.

JACK   Your wife?

HENRY   Yes, she's just upstairs preening herself. You know what women are.

JACK   I suppose so.

HENRY   Of course you do. A handsome young man like you. You know women. Now, here we are . . .

(HENRY *almost manhandles* JACK *and places him in front of the fire.*)

	Warm yourself. (HENRY *stands back and admires the scene. Beat.*) Put more wood on the fire if you want.
JACK	No, no, this is just lovely, thank you, Mr Roth.
HENRY	And enough of that. It's Henry.
JACK	Right.
HENRY	Try it.
JACK	I'm sorry?
HENRY	Say it.
JACK	Erm . . . Henry.
HENRY	Excellent.

(*Pause.* JACK *feels slightly 'observed'.*)

	How was the journey?
JACK	Fine, thank you. The Euston train was on time and really quite quiet. Most people got off at Glasgow.
HENRY	Did they, the poor things. And the valley bus?
JACK	Yes, fine. I mean, it wasn't really running on time but it turned up eventually.
HENRY	It's a law unto itself.
JACK	Evidently.
HENRY	Was it busy?

JACK   The bus? Not really, a handful of people, that's all.

HENRY   A handful? That's rush hour.

             (*Pause. Again, awkward for* JACK.)

JACK   But I got here.

HENRY   You did. Yes. (*Beat.*) A drink? What can I get you? We have all sorts really. Wine, red and white. Whisky, gin. Vodka. There's some brandy somewhere, though I don't touch the stuff myself. Heartburn.

JACK   Ah.

HENRY   But yes . . . any of the above.

JACK   Have you got a beer?

HENRY   A beer? God, I don't know. A beer? I shouldn't have thought so.

JACK   Oh, well don't worry. I'll just have a . . . what are you having?

HENRY   Well, I was having whisky but really, you ought to have what you want to have.

JACK   Whisky will be fine.

HENRY   No, no. Let's wait and see if we have any beer. I'm afraid you're asking the wrong person. My wife . . . we'll ask her when she comes down.

JACK   I hope she's not going to too much trouble.

HENRY	Me too. (*Beat.*) How marvellous. To have you here. In my house. Truly wonderful.
JACK	It's very kind of you to have me. I really am very excited. It's a big deal for me.
HENRY	Good, I'm pleased. I'm just glad you made it.
JACK	How do you mean?
HENRY	You may have been got.
JACK	I don't quite follow.
HENRY	By 'The Ghoul'. We were just laughing about it when you arrived.
JACK	The Ghoul? Oh . . . yes of course. The murderer.
HENRY	The marauding madman. Slicing up his victims in the country's most picturesque locations. The tourist boards will be in meltdown!
JACK	Yes, I suppose. I picked up a paper on the train and read about it. Awful business really.
HENRY	Not for a thriller writer.
JACK	No, no I guess not. One man's tragedy is another man's inspiration.
HENRY	Well said.
JACK	But isn't it funny how we assume things.
HENRY	In what way?

JACK   You just assume he's a man.

HENRY   Do I?

JACK   Yes. You said . . . slicing up *his* victims.

HENRY   (*resting on the arm of the settee*) Yes, I did. How perceptive of you. No wonder you're such a talented actor.

JACK   But isn't it interesting? When it comes to murderers, psychopaths or whatever else we call them, so often we simply assume that they're male.

HENRY   Well, call me a chauvinist but I can't help but feel that women are too . . . squeamish. For all that gouging and slashing.

JACK   Maybe. So how do you think a woman would murder?

HENRY   That's easy. She'd make us fall in love with her.

JACK   Yes.

HENRY   (*eases himself up with his stick and moves over to the table. He picks up the brown envelope and inspects it*) Still, although I'm sure 'The Ghoul' is many miles away by now . . . moved onto the next natural beauty spot no doubt . . . it does add a certain piquancy to tonight's events.

JACK   Tonight's events?

HENRY   Yes, tonight's murder.

          (*Beat.*)

JACK	I'm afraid you've lost me.
HENRY	(*throwing the envelope down and picking up the script*) The play, my dear, Jack! The play!
	(*They laugh together.*)
JACK	Yes, yes of course. You had me worried for a moment.
HENRY	Worried? What on earth would you be worried about?
JACK	I didn't put two and two together. When you mentioned murder, well . . . with all this talk about The Ghoul and what have you. Well . . .
HENRY	You let your imagination run away with you.
JACK	Something like that.
HENRY	You allowed your fears to take hold.
JACK	Maybe not *fears*, uncertainties perhaps.
HENRY	I see. You thought for a moment that I was he.
JACK	Who?
HENRY	The Ghoul.
JACK	Ha! No, no. That didn't cross my mind. I don't see you as a murderer, Mr Roth.
HENRY	No?
JACK	I don't think so.
HENRY	But I could easily become one.

JACK	Oh?
HENRY	If you persist in calling me Mr Roth.
JACK	Oh, Henry. Yes, of course.
HENRY	That's right. Now relax. This isn't a job interview. Or worse, an audition. I've seen you on stage, remember.
JACK	You said so on the phone. At the Royal Court.
HENRY	Precisely. The Royal Court. How grand.
JACK	I'm glad you enjoyed it.
HENRY	I didn't. Hated every minute of it. Except your performance.
JACK	It was really a very small part.
HENRY	No such thing as small parts . . .
JACK	. . . Only small actors.
HENRY	Precisely!
JACK	(*seeing the poster on the wall*) Oh, wow! "Bloodlust". Hey, I remember this. I went to see it on tour. Mum and dad took me when I was a kid.
HENRY	A kid? Really.
JACK	Ah, it was great. I loved that bit at the end with the wife screaming as the gunman enters the house. She thinks it's her husband or something.

HENRY	The other way around in fact. Her husband enters the house and she thinks it's the gunman.
JACK	That's right! Yeah, and she shoots him and then finds out she's shot her husband and it all goes wrong and he's crawling about with blood all over himself trying to tell her where the gunman actually is.
HENRY	Yes, I happen to know the plot.
JACK	Fantastic. Didn't they make it for TV afterwards? I'm sure I caught some of it one afternoon. You know how they constantly repeat these tired old shows. (*Beat.*) Oh, hell. I didn't mean . . . I'm sorry. I wasn't meaning . . .
HENRY	Don't worry. I'm of the same opinion. I never watch it myself.
JACK	Well, no. You must be sick of it. Still, do you reckon this new one will be as good?
HENRY	Better.
JACK	Oh fantastic. My parents'll love to come and see me in it. They came to the Royal Court but all my father said was "I didn't understand a bloody word of it."
HENRY	I think I'd get on with your father.
	(JACK *inspects the poster again, admiringly.*)
JACK	Halliwell!
HENRY	I'm sorry?

JACK	The murderer in "Bloodlust". That's his name, Halliwell.
HENRY	Yes, I know.
JACK	Of course. (*He laughs at himself.*) So, are we going to read from the play?
HENRY	Which play?
JACK	This new one, the one you want me to be in. You do still want me for the part?
HENRY	More than ever.
JACK	Thank God for that. So I can tell my agent?
HENRY	Well, it's a little late, don't you think? All the agents I know are in some swanky wine bar by now lying to their clients about how wonderful they are.
JACK	But in the morning. I can tell her that I've got the part.
HENRY	You didn't tell her you were coming here?
JACK	No, no. Just as you asked. I kept it to myself. Not even my flatmate knows. He thinks I've gone to Manchester for a physical theatre workshop.
HENRY	Good God.
JACK	That nearly backfired though, he wanted to come too.
HENRY	An actor himself, is he?
JACK	He likes to think so.

HENRY	Oh, you bitch.

JACK   That was mean, wasn't it?

HENRY Spoken like a true actor. But in answer to your original question, no I don't think we will read directly from the script. I'm not sure if I'm ready for that yet. And there's nothing worse than a writer directing his own work. No, I think tonight's proceedings will take the form of, shall we say . . . roleplay. If that doesn't sound too dreadful.

JACK   Whatever you think is best.

HENRY Excellent. Now, did you bring what we talked about?

JACK   I did.

HENRY Well, come on, dear boy. Show me, show me.

(HENRY *pushes the script and envelope to one side to clear some space on the coffee table.* JACK *collects his back from the window seat and brings it down stage.*)

JACK   I hope it's okay. I mean, I hope it's what you wanted.

HENRY There's no right or wrong. It's just a little exercise. Do you remember what I asked?

JACK   Of course. To bring three items that could be described as the essential props of a murderer.

HENRY Very good. I want to see that you can think like a killer. See inside the mind of a

	psychopath. This is very important if you're going to play one.
JACK	Yes, of course.
HENRY	And this is why casting the role is so vital. You almost have to be the opposite of what a killer should look like. Act like, even. Psychopaths are never noticed for anything until they are caught. They blend in. It is only their private thoughts, their easy acceptance of evil that sets them apart.
JACK	Right.
HENRY	So come on. Your three items.

(HENRY *sits down in an armchair and waits expectantly as* JACK *opens his bag. He pulls out a toothbrush.*)

	Well, that's rather disappointing.
JACK	That's not one of them. That's just my toothbrush.
HENRY	I can see that.
JACK	Sorry, but as I'm staying the night . . . you know.
HENRY	Don't worry. Although one can assume even psychopaths have a sense of duty towards their oral hygiene.
JACK	Yes, quite.

(JACK *puts the toothbrush away. He rummages again and this time comes out with a pair of black leather gloves.*)

HENRY	Interesting.
JACK	It may be a little clichéd, but I am guessing fingerprints are still foremost on a killer's mind.
HENRY	Excellent, yes. And black leather. How wonderfully Hitchcock.
JACK	That's what I thought.
HENRY	And next?

(JACK *places the gloves on the table and then from the bag pulls out a length of rope and lets it unfurl.*)

JACK	I'm afraid Hitchcock is in the room again.
HENRY	Explain this one to me.
JACK	Well, it serves two purposes, really. Firstly, of course, it's a weapon. Strangulation is a slow and, one assumes, enjoyable method of killing someone. You can actually watch the life drain from your victim's eyes.
HENRY	Very good.
JACK	Secondly, it's a form of restraint. Giving you a real sense of control. Of total power.
HENRY	Making the victim power-*less*.
JACK	Precisely.
HENRY	Fabulous. Just imagine how that would feel.
JACK	Yes. Imagine.

HENRY And thirdly . . . ?

(JACK *curls the rope onto the table. Then from the bag pulls out a rather large and terrifying looking knife. This is not the sort of knife you can buy in a kitchenware shop.*)

HENRY Bloody hell.

JACK I wondered whether you wanted me to source one of those prop knives, like the ones you use on stage . . . but then I thought, that's thinking like an actor, not a killer. So why not bring the real thing?

HENRY Well, I'm glad you didn't fly up here. Security would have had a field day.

JACK Is it a bit too much?

HENRY Far from it, my dear boy, far from it. It's quite perfect. Really it is.

JACK You see, we're talking about a psychopath aren't we? In this play, this character is not committing a crime of passion, I guess.

HENRY No, certainly not.

JACK Exactly. The killer *enjoys* the act of taking someone's life. And this knife, I feel, represents a psychopath who treats what he does as an art form. Something to be done with skill, patience and . . . well . . . care.

HENRY Care?

JACK Yes. Not for the victim. But for the art of murder itself.

(JACK *approaches* HENRY *with the knife.*)

The killer sees himself as a skilled craftsman, a rare breed of man that has the unique ability not only to take another man's life – anyone can do that – but as a man capable of making the death of a fellow man artful, precise, beautiful.

(JACK *is now in a very threatening position over* HENRY, *who is not sure where this is going. The blade is resting on* HENRY'S *chest. They stare at one another for a moment.* JACK *leans in very close to* HENRY.)

HENRY The part is definitely yours.

(*They smile at one another.* EVELYN *appears at the top of the stairs and on seeing the scene in front of she screams.* JACK *leaps away in shock, the knife dangerously close to* HENRY.)

HENRY For God's sake, Evelyn . . . you could have got me killed!

EVELYN (*making her way down stairs*) What the hell's going on?

HENRY Roleplay, Evelyn! Roleplay! I wouldn't expect you to understand.

EVELYN Well I'm sorry, but you must admit it looked a little odd.

HENRY Looks can be deceiving. You of all people should know that.

(HENRY *rises from the armchair.* JACK *has his back to* EVELYN *and is seemingly stunned into stillness. As if he can't believe something he's heard.*)

EVELYN As awkward as this is, don't you think you should introduce me to your . . . murderer?

HENRY Why of course. How rude of me. Evelyn, may I present my latest muse and the lead in my soon-to-be-smash-hit play, "Death Knell" . . . Mr Jack Willoughby.

(JACK *turns around, slowly. Pause.*)

Well, well. Struck dumb by his beauty, are we? You must be used to this, Jack. Forgive her, she has only me as male company these days I rather pale into an invisible blandness when in your company. I'll do her job for her. Jack, my wife . . . Evelyn.

JACK Yes. Right. Hello, pleased to meet you. Evelyn. (*He goes to shake her hand, realises he still has the knife in his hand.*) Oh, sorry. Rather inappropriate. I don't usually carry such things, I promise. (*He places the knife on the table.*)

EVELYN I'm pleased to hear it.

(*They greet one another, awkwardly. They're not sure whether a kiss would be appropriate and rather clumsily opt for a handshake instead.*)

It's a pleasure to meet you . . . Jack, is it?

JACK That's right. Likewise. I'm sorry, I didn't know I was disturbing your evening.

EVELYN	You're not. I mean . . . well . . . what I saw as I came down the stairs was pretty disturbing but apart from that . . .
JACK	Good. Right.
	(*Pause.*)
	(*Over one another suddenly . . .*)
JACK	I must admit I didn't –
EVELYN	So, how was the journey, it's –
EVELYN	Sorry, you go ahead.
JACK	No, you, please.
EVELYN	I was wondering if your journey was all right.
JACK	Yes, fine. Thank you. Quiet really. After Glasgow, anyway.
EVELYN	Yes, everyone gets off at Glasgow.
HENRY	That's what Jack said. Wasn't it, Jack?
JACK	Mm? Yes. Everyone does.
EVELYN	Have you ever been?
JACK	To Glasgow? No.
EVELYN	You should. Worth a visit. Good shops.
JACK	Right. Thanks.
	(*Pause.* HENRY *goes to stoke the fire.*)

EVELYN	What were going to say?
JACK	When?
EVELYN	Earlier. I interrupted you.
HENRY	Hardly interrupted. You spoke at the same time. In sync, almost.
JACK	Erm . . . just that, well, I didn't know Mr Roth was married. I mean, I didn't know you'd be here. His wife.
EVELYN	Ah. He never talked about me?
JACK	Never.
HENRY	Jack, *Jack* . . . you're going to get me into trouble. You'll have my wife thinking I don't mention her to anyone.
JACK	It just never came up, I suppose. It never occurred to me.
HENRY	Ah, well that's a totally different matter. It never *occurred* to you. Do you hear that, Evelyn? It never occurred to him that I would be married. I think I know what he's getting at. (HENRY *makes his way across the room, collecting his glass and begins to pour himself another drink.*) I really shouldn't. Evelyn will tell you. I have the terrible propensity to drink far too much of an evening. But hopefully tonight she'll refrain from reprimanding me in front of a guest. Darling?
EVELYN	Do what you want.

HENRY	Ha! A sentence I haven't heard in a while. But a philosophy I think we all should adhere to. Jack?
JACK	No, thank you.
HENRY	Oh, that's right. You wanted a beer. Darling, do we have any beer for young Jack?
EVELYN	I shouldn't think so, I haven't bought any.
HENRY	So . . . . I'm afraid, no beer.
JACK	That's quite all right. Thank you.

(HENRY *pours himself his whisky.*)

HENRY	I do wish you two would sit down. It's like having Stonehenge in the living room.

(*They don't move.*)

Sit, sit. Come on. We suddenly have a less than convivial atmosphere. And all because my wife caught me being threatened at knifepoint by a psychopathic killer.

(JACK *and* EVELYN *have sat down on opposite armchairs.*)

JACK	I wasn't actually threatening him. It was . . .
EVELYN	Roleplay, yes.

(HENRY *takes his drink and stands in between them both, centre of the room.*)

HENRY	Lovely. Funny, how we assume things, though. Jack was just saying that earlier. Weren't you, Jack?

JACK · I'm sorry?

HENRY · Yes, Jack and I were talking about this Ghoul, chap. And Jack, quite rightly, picked up on the fact that I just assumed that he was in fact a he. Who's to say this Ghoul isn't a woman? Evelyn?

EVELYN · I . . . I don't know. Perhaps women aren't capable of such things.

HENRY · Perhaps. Or perhaps women are just too damn clever for their own good. Perhaps women have far more deceitful, slippery, subtle ways of stopping the beating of a human heart. What do you think?

(*No answer.*)

Interesting. And again, sorry to keep using you as an example, but young Jack here just assumed I wasn't married. It was entirely my own fault. I didn't mention my wife. I neglected to say, "Jack, I am married".

EVELYN · Henry, don't go on . . .

HENRY · And therefore, Jack, neither did it cross your mind that the woman you have been sleeping with for six months is in fact, my wife.

(HENRY *drains his glass. Silence.*)

What? Nothing, not even a squeak?

EVELYN · I don't know what you're talking about.

HENRY · Predictably dull response. Jack?

JACK · I . . . I don't quite understand.

HENRY	Dear me. All beauty but no brains. You're screwing my wife, Jack.
JACK	This is absurd.
HENRY	He speaks! And why is this absurd, dear boy? On what level could this possibly be absurd? As far as I can tell this is perfectly, tragically real.
JACK	But . . . I didn't know. I promise. I had no clue.
HENRY	Objection, your honour! Weak defence. Lacks substance. The term, 'that's no excuse' springs to mind, not to mention the sheer cowardice of refusing to take any responsibility. I don't particularly admire my wife at the moment but even I know that she's only one half of the guilty party. Try again.
EVELYN	Fine. If you want to play this out like some sort of pathetic courtroom drama, where's your proof?
HENRY	At last, a salient question. Exhibit A.
	(HENRY *takes the contents from the envelope. A series of photographs. He spreads them out and using the end of his cane pushes them towards* EVELYN *and* JACK.)
EVELYN	How . . . ? But you were . . . ?
HENRY	Seeing my agent? I only said that in case someone inadvertently let slip that I went to London that week. People in the town see things and worse, they talk. We all need a cover story occasionally.

JACK: Oh, God.

HENRY: I am sorry for lying my love, but then again, you were meant to be at the clinic. So both our covers have been blown. We'd make lousy criminals, wouldn't we?

JACK: That's us. That's my flat.

HENRY: And a foul little broom cupboard it is, Jack. Where was it again . . . Peckham? Insalubrious place for a romantic getaway, but each to their own.

EVELYN: You followed us . . . you actually spied on us like . . . like . . .

HENRY: Like a cuckold? A betrayed and broken man who has given his wife all she could ever want and yet she still shacks up with some brainless twit in a flea-ridden drug den! Like that perhaps?

JACK: But how?

HENRY: Because when my wife first visited the clinic I made sure that she was unable to run away. That she was safe. I was looking out for my wife's welfare.

EVELYN: Ha!

HENRY: So I made sure, secretly, that when we started on the programme of her attending the clinic every six weeks, I would get a phone call from them once she had checked in.

EVELYN: You did what?

HENRY	At first it all went perfectly. I would drop her at the station and later that night I would hear that she was there safe, and sound. My mind was put to rest. But then, about six months ago, these phone calls stopped. When I enquired I was told that Mrs Roth herself had cancelled the treatment. So imagine my surprise when I phoned her mobile only to hear this same Mrs Roth say to me that she was happily ensconced at the clinic and all was well. Oh, my first thoughts were that she was off again, on some booze-addled bender, but the woman I was speaking to was perfectly compos mentis. So what the hell was she doing? And where? A few days later she came home full of the stories of the counselling sessions and the breakthroughs she's made. Good God! Well, we both kept up our ends of this merry little pretence. Of course I was all ready to challenge her . . . but instead a finer idea began to form in my head. I decided to play her at her own game. I decided that the next time she went to 'the clinic' I would be right behind her. *Literally.*
EVELYN	You were on the same train?
HENRY	Of course. First class. You wouldn't have noticed.
EVELYN	You sneaky, conniving . . .
HENRY	Before you go on, remember that everything I am, you are too. And worse. Like I told you, I am not a bad man, Evelyn.
JACK	You followed her to my flat?
HENRY	And took the photos you now have in your grubby little hands. May I offer a word of

	advice to you, my lascivious little darlings; it does to close the curtains when passion takes hold. I got the proof I needed far quicker than anticipated and then made a tenuous excuse to visit my agent.
JACK	You mean, there's no play? There's no part for me?
HENRY	Oh, there's a play all right. But there's certainly no part in it for you, you talentless little shit.
JACK	Hey!
HENRY	Hey, nothing! I suppose that's how you met. When he was at the Royal Court on Sloane Square. *Just next door.* Am I right? (*Pause.*) I thought as much. A fleeting glance across the street? Love at first sight? How heart warming. But if you believe for one moment that I am going to bless this union, you're going to be sorely disappointed. My darling wife whom I rescued from the gutter, from the very depths of depravity and even prison . . . you repay me like this.
JACK	Prison?
EVELYN	Jack, please . . .
HENRY	Oh, you don't know? Why do you think I walk with this cursed stick, Jack? It's not a gimmick. This is the handiwork of your beloved, here. She hit me with her uninsured car, when drunk, can you believe. Not a traditional way to meet your future spouse but it worked for us.
EVELYN	It's not how it sounds.

HENRY	It's exactly as it sounds. Evelyn was driving a car she couldn't afford to insure with a belly full of cheap vodka. She hit me as I crossed the road outside of my flat. Fortunately for her it was in the middle of the night and I was the only witness. I knew she had been drink driving, she had that glazed look and stank like the floor of a nightclub. Still, she had the wherewithal to drive me to the nearest hospital and unceremoniously dump me outside A & E. A few days later, wracked with guilt she visited me. She assumed I was going to go to the police and came begging me not to. I promised I wouldn't, as long as she promised to go for dinner with me. Sober. And the rest as they say . . .
JACK	That's insane.
HENRY	(*as he says the following he picks up the leather gloves and puts them on, then takes up the knife*) You cannot understand the fury burning inside of me. The purest anger. And you can't begin to comprehend what I am capable of.
JACK	Henry . . . what the hell are you doing?
EVELYN	This is not the time for your games. Henry!
	(*She moves towards him but he slices the air with the knife and she stops in her tracks. He moves towards* JACK.)
JACK	Listen, I know you must be angry. But I know you're not capable of doing something as stupid as hurting me.

HENRY	I want to do a lot more than just hurt you, Jack my boy.
JACK	This is crazy.

(*He starts to back away from* HENRY.)

HENRY	You should be careful when men you don't know phone you and ask you to their house in the middle of nowhere, Jack. I could have been anyone. A murdering psychopath even.
EVELYN	Henry, stop this!

(EVELYN *runs at* HENRY *who hits her with his stick. She falls to the ground.*)

JACK	Darling!
HENRY	Don't you dare call her that!

(*He dashes at* JACK *with the knife,* JACK *falls over a piece of furniture and is stranded as* HENRY *bears down on him, knife held to strike.*)

JACK	Please, please!
EVELYN	Henry, no!

(HENRY *brings the knife down violently. It lands just to the side of* JACK'S *face. He slowly opens his eyes and realises he is still alive.*)

HENRY	Pathetic. What sort of man are you?

(HENRY *gets back up, walks to the coffee table, chucks the knife on the table and takes off the gloves.* EVELYN *rises to her feet,* JACK *still stunned, manages to do the same.*)

JACK (*approaching* EVELYN) Darling . . .

EVELYN Don't. Please. This isn't right . . . I didn't mean to . . .

JACK Didn't mean to what? Fall in love with me.

(HENRY *snorts.*)

EVELYN I just got carried away. I can't . . . Jack . . . I can't do this.

JACK What the hell are you talking about? We love each other.

EVELYN Don't be so naïve. Don't you see? . . . What we had was secret. It was . . . escapism. God, I loved it, of course I did. But I have Henry. I owe him my life. I owe him . . . all of this.

JACK No, you don't mean that. You can't. Everything we talked about . . .

EVELYN . . . Was make believe.

JACK Not to me.

EVELYN Jack, please.

JACK Oh, for God's sake, Evelyn. No! Only two minutes ago you said you loved me.

EVELYN Did I? What we had could be mistaken for love . . . but it's not. I was in love with what you *signified*. Not with you.

JACK	So that's it? You're just going to stay, with him? He's a freak! A controlling madman. Look at me, I can offer you . . .
EVELYN	What? What can you offer me? Look around you. I would be leaving this. Security, safety, money.
JACK	Love? Because that's what I can give.
EVELYN	Oh, Jack. You're so . . .
JACK	What? What am I, Evelyn?
EVELYN	Young.
	(JACK *approaches* EVELYN *and goes to put his hand on her cheek. She pulls away.*)
	No, Jack . . . please.
JACK	Darling, listen . . .
EVELYN	(*now almost in tears and hastily heading towards the door*) I'm sorry . . . I just . . . I'm sorry.
	(*Finally breaking down she grabs her coat and runs out of the door into the night. We hear the car drive off. Silence.*)
JACK	I'll have that whisky now, if that's okay with you?
HENRY	The medicine of the spurned man. Help yourself.
JACK	(*pouring a drink*) I'll need a lift into town.

HENRY	No can do, I'm afraid. Not only does your beloved have the car but I've had far too many of these. Unlike my wife, I refuse to drink and drive.
JACK	(*slamming down the bottle*) I suppose you think yourself very clever.
HENRY	Clever? Why?
JACK	Getting me all the way up here so you could orchestrate, no, *direct* your dramatic little revelation.
HENRY	Do you really believe that's why I invited you up here? Dear me . . . what's just happened could just as easily have played out in any restaurant in London. No, I invited you up here for something far more important.
JACK	And what's that?
HENRY	I told you when you arrived that all this talk of the Ghoul added a certain piquancy to tonight's murder. Well that's exactly why I invited you here. For murder.
JACK	Say again.
HENRY	This is the perfect spot. Here, in the middle of nowhere, no neighbours for twenty minutes, a deep loch less than fifty yards away and on top of that no one even knows you're here. Don't you see, we are perfectly set up for a murder? I didn't ask you to bring these props for a roleplay, Jack. I asked you to bring them so you could use them.

(*Pause.*)

JACK · You're sick.

HENRY · No, I'm angry. As are you. And that's what murderers need to be.

JACK · And who, may I ask, am I meant to be murdering?

(HENRY *looks towards the door.*)

JACK · Evelyn? Mad! This is mad!

HENRY · Don't write it off until you've heard my terms.

JACK · And why would I want to kill her?

HENRY · Oh, come on! If you do really love her, you must be feeling pretty humiliated right now. A pure rage? Trust me, I know how you feel.

JACK · So you do it.

HENRY · Think, Jack, think. Let's say for argument's sake that suspicions are aroused . . . who is always the first to be investigated? The husband. I don't want to be a murderer if I can help it.

JACK · And the second suspect is always the lover.

HENRY · Perhaps. But how many people know about the affair? If I know Evelyn, she would have made sure to keep it a secret.

JACK · I suppose she did. She even went as far as only ringing me from phone boxes.

HENRY · And she made sure you kept your mouth shut?

JACK	I wasn't to tell anyone. I wanted to, of course. We were worried my flatmate suspected something, he caught us at a café once. It was careless but we fobbed him off with some story about her being an actress I'd met at an audition. He seemed to buy it.
HENRY	But what about the assignations at your flat . . . surely he was there?
JACK	No. He always goes to his girlfriend's at the weekends. It was perfect.
HENRY	So there you go. Nothing whatsoever to connect you to the victim. And quite apart from all this of course, there's the sweetener.
JACK	Sweetener?
HENRY	Indeed. I want you to provide a service, for me. I'm sure you understand that I can't remain married to Evelyn, yet nor can I conceivably suffer the ignominy of divorce. Quite apart from the hideous embarrassment, there's also the matter of the settlement. The courts of this land will insist that I keep her in the style to which she has become accustomed. And that, I'm afraid, is never going to happen. So it seems only fair that I pay you a portion of the money I would otherwise have to give to a cheating, manipulative whore. Acceptable terms, don't you think?
JACK	How much are we talking about?
HENRY	Well, if I may make an assumption. You're an actor and not a very good one. You will be drowning in debt. Am I right? Although

the amount I will give you will be nowhere near the amount I would be forced to give to Evelyn, it'll be more money than you have ever earned and are ever likely to earn.

(HENRY *walks over to the laptop computer.*)

Isn't internet banking a wonderful thing? And quite necessary when you live so far from the nearest branch.

(HENRY *taps the keyboard.*)

Here. Pass me your bank card.

(JACK *takes out a wallet and hands him a bank card.*)

All I have to do is see that your end of the bargain has been upheld and the money will be transferred immediately.

(HENRY *types a series of numbers into the computer and then types the numbers he reads from the bank card.*)

As for the amount, I do hope this proves acceptable.

(JACK *looks at the screen. He is slightly taken aback.*)

All it takes is the click of a button and you'll be a rich young man.

(*Pause.* JACK *wrestles with the idea.*)

JACK I've seen this play, Henry. Man pays other man to do his dirty work for him. Kill his

	wife. It all seems foolproof but it all goes wrong in the end.

HENRY　　　Of course you've seen that play. I've written a version of it. But this isn't make believe. It's simple, watertight and it'll work. Trust me. I make a living from thinking like this.

JACK　　　You want me to do it tonight?

HENRY　　　Tonight. She'll be back, she always comes back. Once it's done, put the body into the rowing boat moored in our boathouse and take it into the middle of the loch; it's one of the deepest in Scotland. Even if suspicions do fall anywhere near here, no diver will find her once she's resting on the bottom. You've brought all the right props, now all you have to do is use them wisely.

(JACK *goes to the coffee table and puts on the leather gloves, takes up the knife and the rope. He collects his backpack and makes to the door.*)

I suggest hiding in the boathouse for the time being.

JACK　　　And where will you be?

HENRY　　　Where do you think? I know what's coming, I'll be sure to be out of the way.

JACK　　　I want the money transferred straight away.

HENRY　　　You have my word.

(JACK *decides upon doing it and opens the front door to leave.*)

HENRY	Jack. You're not thinking. Your jacket.
	(JACK *sees his jacket on the coat stand and takes it, putting it on.*)
	Keep a cool head. Murder is easy. It's getting away with it that's the trick.
	(JACK *exits, shutting the door behind him.* HENRY *goes to the window and watches him leave; we hear his feet on the gravel disappear into silence.* HENRY *turns most of the lights out before going to the settee and sitting down. A moment later we hear a car approaching, the headlights ghosting through the room once again. Engine dies, footsteps approaching. The door opens and* EVELYN *enters. She hangs up her coat. She doesn't see* HENRY *and looks up the stairs before stealthily going to the drinks table and pouring a whisky. She looks at the glass of liquor for a moment.*)
	Has it really come to that?
EVELYN	(*screams and drops the glass*) Henry? What are you doing? Where's Jack?
HENRY	Missing him already?
EVELYN	Why, where is he? Henry . . . what have you done?
HENRY	Don't worry, I haven't. Tempting as it was. He left. I thought you might have seen him on the road. He's got a long walk back.
	(*Pause.* EVELYN *stares out of the window.*)

I'm off to bed. Alone. I don't care where exactly you sleep, but if you insist on drinking yourself into a stupor tonight, I don't suppose you care either.

(HENRY *rises from the settee and approaches* EVELYN.)

Let me look at you.

(*He stares at her, intensely. She stares back.*)

Goodnight.

(HENRY *makes his way up the stairs.* EVELYN *decides not to have a drink and takes the glass she dropped into the kitchen. Then, very quietly, we hear footsteps approaching the house. They stop as* EVELYN *returns from the kitchen. She thinks she sees something out of the window. She shivers and closes the curtains. Then she goes to the phone and dials a number.*)

EVELYN (*hushed*) Jack, I know you won't have any signal, but I just wanted to leave a message anyway. Call me a coward. I don't know what to say . . . One day, I hope you understand. Thank you, for . . . I'll miss you. (*She hangs up and as she puts the phone down, she spots* JACK'S *bank card on the desk. Bemused, she picks it up and studies it, walking towards the stairs to ask* HENRY *about it. Suddenly a knocking at the front door. She jumps.*) Jack?

(*Scared, she summons the courage and opens the front door quickly. No one there. She closes it before walking backwards away from door. Beat.* JACK *jumps out from the kitchen and immediately wraps the rope around her neck to strangle her.* EVELYN *drops the bank card [**to end up under the settee – place during interval**]. A struggle ensues.* EVELYN *manages to elbow* JACK *in the stomach and get free, but he trips her up. He pulls out the knife and brings it down but she avoids it, struggles to her knees, kicks* JACK *in the face.*)

EVELYN Henry! Henry! Help!

(*She runs to the front door and opens it, but* JACK *recovers in time to stagger towards her and force the door closed. He swipes at her with the knife and catches her arm, she screams in pain, holding the wound tight.* JACK *approaches her slowly, knife aloft. At the last moment* EVELYN *darts out of the way, scrabbles over to the rope. As he dashes after her she leaps up and wraps the rope around his throat. She uses all her might to strangle the life out of* JACK, *who eventually ends up hanging over an arm of the settee. He stops moving and drops the knife, which* EVELYN *picks up and studies. She staggers away from the body, almost dreamlike.* HENRY *appears at the top of the stairs. She sees him.*)

Henry . . . ?

(*Suddenly, with a roar,* JACK *jumps up towards* EVELYN. *Almost as a kneejerk reaction, she plunges the knife into his stomach. He grabs the knife, blood appears. He staggers forwards;* EVELYN *pulls away as he collapses onto the centre of the rug. Dead.* HENRY *comes down the stairs.*)

	Why . . . ? I don't understand . . . he was trying to kill me.
HENRY	Oh, my darling! My darling . . . don't you see? He was willing to kill you. It was all my idea. A test. Look at me, Evelyn. Look at me. He didn't love you. I will look after you now. I'll keep you safe.

(*He kisses her.*)

Now come on . . . we need to get the body out of here. Put it in the boat and take him out to the centre of the loch.

(*She doesn't move.*)

Evelyn! Listen! You need to do this. I can't. You need to drop his body into the loch, weighed down. No one even knows he's here. But we have to get on with it, now. Go . . . go!

(HENRY *opens the front door wide.*)

I'll go and gather rocks from the shore. Wrap him in something. The rug. And use the rope to tie it up. Put the knife back in his pocket. It all has to disappear, you understand? Do you understand?

(EVELYN *nods.*)

Good. Evelyn. I love you. Everything will be fine. You'll see.

(HENRY *exits.* EVELYN *shakily places the knife and rope back in* JACK's *pockets fighting off tears. She gathers herself.*

Inspects her knife wound. Stands and stares at the body. The clock marks the hour.

Lights dim.

End of Act One.)

ACT TWO

A month later. It is nearly Christmas. The scene is as Act One except that the drinks table has now gone, as has the rug. "Carols from King's" plays softly from the library.

It is 5 p.m. and darkness is encroaching upon the house. Outside it is freezing cold. The clock marks the time in its usual way.

HENRY enters from the library.

HENRY	Evelyn? (*He shouts up the stairs . . .*) Evelyn? (*He pokes his head into the kitchen; she's not there. He then looks out of the window towards the loch and sighs. Opens the front door.*) Evelyn! Evelyn, for God's sake, it's freezing out there. Come in.
	(*He re-enters the house and a few moments later is followed by a frozen* EVELYN.)
	You should have taken a coat at least. You'll catch your death. Evelyn?
EVELYN	I like the cold. It makes you numb.
HENRY	Don't be ridiculous. I haven't the energy to look after you if you get the flu.
EVELYN	No. I don't suppose you do. (*She takes off her coat, winces as she removes her wounded arm.*)
HENRY	How is it today?
EVELYN	I don't think it's any better.

HENRY	Of course it is. That's what the body does. It gets better.
EVELYN	Not mine. It's a reminder.
HENRY	Here, let me have a look. (*He approaches her but she backs away.*) Oh, Evelyn, come on.
EVELYN	The only person who should look at it is a doctor.
HENRY	We're not going over this again.
EVELYN	It could be infected.
HENRY	It was a deep wound, these things take a while.
EVELYN	I know how deep it was, Henry. Of all people, I know.
HENRY	Yes . . . of course. Just give it time.
EVELYN	What if I'm dying? What if I have some sort of blood infection pulsing through my body?
HENRY	You're being ridiculous.
EVELYN	I need to see a doctor.
HENRY	You can't go to the doctor. What would you tell him? They have protocols you know. He could tell straight away it was a knife wound and alarm bells would ring. First about you . . . I don't know . . . self-harming. And then onto me attacking you and before we know it they have somehow connected us to the

	disappearance of that young man in London whom no one has seen in a month.
EVELYN	What? But you promised me . . .
HENRY	I did. And I still do. No one will suspect a thing as long as we're careful. And going to the doctor is not being careful. You have to trust me, Evelyn.
EVELYN	Is that what you call this? Trust. Not letting me out of the house on my own. Keeping the car keys locked away. Shouting for me every other minute to see where I am.
HENRY	I call it love.
EVELYN	I call it blackmail!
HENRY	Excuse me?
EVELYN	Don't you see, you have something over me all over again. For years it was the car accident. And now it's this. (*Suddenly moving.*) Oh, I hate these bloody carols!
	(*She marches into the library and the carols stop playing abruptly. She re-enters the room, gathering herself.*)
HENRY	I want you to calm down.
EVELYN	I want a drink.
HENRY	I'm sure you do. But there's none in the house.
EVELYN	Yes. I know.

HENRY	It's all for your own good. I'm protecting you.
	(EVELYN *reacts to this*.)
	But I am! You're a murderer, Evelyn. And the only person in the world who knows that, is me.
EVELYN	And you're loving every minute of it.
HENRY	That's unkind. You're tired. You're not sleeping, you're hardly eating. And you're taking it out on me.
EVELYN	And who else am I meant to take it out on? Tell me that? I talk to no one else. I hardly see anyone except for a trip into town, with you right by my side. You don't even let me answer the damn phone!
HENRY	Well if you were behaving a little more rationally . . .
EVELYN	Rationally? What's rational about any of this? I killed a man. I rowed him into the middle of a loch and I dropped his body over the side! Tell me, Henry. What's rational about any of that?
HENRY	Nothing. I know. But now we have to behave as if nothing has happened and if you can't even do that with me, how on earth am I meant to trust you to do it with other people?
EVELYN	I can't shake it off. This feeling. It is . . . engrained within me that I'm a murderer. And this . . . (*She indicates the wound on her arm.*) This just serves to remind me.

	That's why I know, it will never heal. (*Beat. She goes to say something else but stops herself.*) Oh, what's the point . . . ?
HENRY	What?
	(*Pause.*)
EVELYN	I keep seeing him.
HENRY	I'm sorry?
EVELYN	Jack. I keep seeing him.
HENRY	What, in your head?
EVELYN	It doesn't feel like it . . . but perhaps. He's there whenever I close my eyes. If I fall asleep his voice wakes me up. But lately I've seen him . . . in person.
HENRY	Oh. Okay.
EVELYN	I knew you wouldn't understand.
HENRY	That's not fair. I do. Of course I do. You've been under a lot of stress. It's no wonder you're having . . . visions.
EVELYN	Visions? I like that. *Visions.*
HENRY	Or whatever you want to call them.
EVELYN	I see him. Everywhere. I catch him in the corner of my eye, passing out of sight as I turn to look. Staring at me through a crowd. Only the other day . . . in town I saw him on the other side of the street. He was there for only a second, if that, but I could see him looking at me with such . . . hate . . .

	such venom. Do you remember? I stopped dead in my tracks and you asked what was wrong but I couldn't tell you. Because when I turned to look again. He'd gone.
HENRY	Yes, I remember. But you must understand, it's all from inside your head. The moment you learn to rid yourself of the guilt, the moment these things will stop happening.
EVELYN	And here . . . in this house.
HENRY	What do you mean?
EVELYN	Oh, Henry, it was dreadful! I was asleep down here on the settee. It was very late and you'd gone to bed. I felt a cold breeze against my legs, I thought about getting up to fetch a blanket but I was too tired to care. And then, suddenly, his face popped into my head. And then a voice, his voice . . . I managed to open my eyes and lift my head from the cushion . . . and . . . he was there! Right there, standing by the fireplace. With that same look of hate. I screamed and ran to turn the lights on, but by the time I had . . . he'd gone. There was no one there.
HENRY	Of course there wasn't, darling.
EVELYN	But the strangest thing of all was that I could smell him. His scent . . . it was still lingering in the room. As if he had been here, watching me sleep all that time.

(*Pause. A bang from upstairs. They jump.*)

HENRY	God! I forgot to shut my bedroom window. The door must have slammed in the draught.

	(*He goes to the stairs and turns.*) Evelyn, sit down. Try to forget these things.
EVELYN	But what if he's haunting me?
HENRY	Then we'll turn all the lights out, sit down, have a séance and tell him very politely to bugger off.
EVELYN	I'm serious.
HENRY	Darling, it's your mind playing tricks. No such thing as hauntings.

(HENRY *walks up the stairs to the bedrooms to shut the window.* EVELYN *walks to the window and stares out, hugging herself. Silence. The door to the library slowly shuts. "Carols from King's" suddenly begins to play again.* EVELYN *turns around, unnerved. She approaches the library door and tentatively puts her hand on the knob. She suddenly flings the door open . . . nothing.*)

EVELYN	Oh, for goodness sake.

(*She hurriedly enters the room and stops the music. She re-enters, looks over to the window above the desk and lets out a piercing scream.* HENRY *comes rushing down the stairs.*)

HENRY	Evelyn!
EVELYN	There . . . he was there . . .
HENRY	What on earth are you talking about?
EVELYN	There was someone at the window.

| HENRY | Darling . . . |

| EVELYN | It was him. |

| HENRY | All right, all right. Come on, sit down. Breathe.

(*He assists her to the settee and she sits, shaking.* HENRY *tentatively goes to the window above the desk and looks out.*)

Well, there's certainly nobody there now. Are you sure it wasn't someone else? |

| EVELYN | Who? Tell me who else would be there? |

| HENRY | God . . . I don't know . . . I'm just trying . . . (*He goes to the front door. Opens it and steps outside.*) |

| EVELYN | Don't! Don't leave me here. |

| HENRY | I'm not leaving you. I'm just taking a look. (HENRY *looks both ways, briefly leaving view. Coming back in and closing front door.*) It's freezing out there. Even the gravel is frozen solid. |

| EVELYN | Anything? |

| HENRY | Nothing. Here, let's warm you up. (HENRY *goes and stokes the fire, and places another log on it. Pause. He looks at his wife.*) Are you absolutely sure you saw something? |

| EVELYN | Not something. Him. |

| HENRY | Evelyn, for God's sake! I watched as you put his body into the loch. You've got to calm |

down. (HENRY *gathers himself.*) Tell me, what can I do to help?

EVELYN　　Undo it. Undo it all.

HENRY　　I see. You're blaming me.

(*She doesn't respond.*)

It's not my fault. We're both victims.

(*Still nothing from her. He snaps . . .*)

You killed him, Evelyn. Not me.

(*She slowly fixes him with her gaze.*)

I'm sorry. That was cruel. Now, I was going to save this for later, I don't know why. But maybe this will help. In some small way. I want you to know how much I trust you.

(*He walks over to the desk . . . He opens a drawer with a key and takes out a bank statement and a bank card. He shuts the drawer but doesn't lock it.* EVELYN *watches all of this. He sits next to her on the settee.*)

This arrived the other day.

(*She takes the card and statement.*)

I promised that I would look after you. I know I've been overbearing at times. As misguided as it may have seemed, it was all out of love. But this is a sign of how much I want you to have your own life, alongside your life with me.

EVELYN　　A bank account?

HENRY

In your name. Only yours. I asked my chap in London to open it for you. Of course, at first, I will transfer money into it but maybe, when you're feeling stronger, you can get a job, I don't know, in town or even work from home. Either way, it's yours and you have your own money now. I want us to be together. And I want you to know that I trust you.

(*She kisses him.*)

EVELYN

Thank you. You don't know what this means.

HENRY

You're welcome. Now, I'll make us both a cup of tea, isn't that what we do to solve all problems?

EVELYN

You're making tea? That's a first.

HENRY

Hey . . . I'm the modern man now.

(*He makes his way into the kitchen.* EVELYN *stands, looking at the bank card and statement. She struggles to hide her delight. She wanders over to the desk and looks out of the window again. Nothing there. She stares out . . .*)

EVELYN

(*seemingly to herself*) Now, come on. Come on.

(*She places the bank card and statement on the desk. As she does this she notices that the drawer is unlocked. She slides it open, mischievously . . . she notices something at the bottom of the drawer. She takes out a small bundle of letters in envelopes. Checking that* HENRY *isn't coming back, she opens one of them and reads. Panicked, she reads another and then another . . . she can barely stand as* HENRY *enters from kitchen with two mugs of tea.*)

HENRY   Does it make me a dreadful husband that I don't know how you take your tea? (*He notices what she's holding.*) Evelyn? What are you doing? That's private.

EVELYN   These letters . . . what are they . . . ?

HENRY   (*placing the mugs down*) Now, calm down. Why do you think I was hiding them?

EVELYN   I have no idea. What the hell are they?

HENRY   I was hiding them because I knew you'd react like this.

EVELYN   How do you expect me to react? They're blackmail letters, Henry!

HENRY   We don't know that.

EVELYN   (*reading one*) "You can't hide what you've done forever." (*And another.*) "Someone knows of your crimes."

HENRY   Yes, yes I've read them . . .

EVELYN   (*reading the next letter*) "I'll see you soon. The truth will come to the surface."

HENRY   Evelyn, stop . . .

EVELYN   "Come to the surface"! The *surface* . . . don't you see? Someone knows. Someone knows what we did.

HENRY   Really? Or are you just reading into things?

EVELYN And what else would they be talking about, Henry, tell me?

HENRY I don't know. Something in the past. The fact that I didn't report you when you hit me with the car. A jilted lover. How would I know?

EVELYN They're talking about the murder!

HENRY They don't actually mention the murder though, do they? For all we know it's just some crazed fan writing to me, trying to get my attention or give me another plot.

EVELYN For God's sake, Henry. You're a thriller writer, not a rock star. Thriller writers don't have crazed fans!

HENRY My point is, it could be anything. It's easy to read into it but we could be . . . we would be . . . very wrong.

EVELYN And why are they addressed to . . . *Halliwell & Partner?* What does that mean?

HENRY Well, that's the thing, someone's got the wrong address. It's just a huge coincidence.

EVELYN Don't be so stupid.

HENRY Then it's just a prank being played.

EVELYN On who?

HENRY Well, me probably. This is why I hid them from you. You were already panicking and if you knew about the letters it would just make things worse.

EVELYN	Well it has, hasn't it? We're being blackmailed by someone and they know what we did.
HENRY	How could anyone know? Tell me that. There was no one around when we did it. No one knew he was coming here. No one has even come and asked us questions about it. As far as anyone is concerned he's just another missing person from London. It happens every day. We've got nothing to worry about.
EVELYN	Yes we do . . . I'm holding it in my hands!
HENRY	(*snatching the letters from her*) Now listen! These letters don't mean a thing. It's probably Andrew playing a joke on me. You know what he's like. He may be a great agent but he's got a terrible sense of humour. I'll phone him after Christmas and get it out of him.
EVELYN	(*suddenly remembering*) Halliwell! That's the name of the murderer in "Bloodlust". *Halliwell & Partner.* Don't you see . . . we've been found out!
HENRY	No. It's just a Christmas joke done in bad taste. If someone really suspected something don't you think the police would be here by now sniffing about?
EVELYN	"I'll see you soon."
HENRY	What?
EVELYN	One of them says, "I'll see you soon." They're going to come here, they're going

	to confront us. I know they are. They're going to take everything from us.
HENRY	Evelyn, stop this! There's no evidence that we've done anything and there's no one coming here. Right? No one is coming here.
	(*Suddenly, a loud knocking on the door. After the initial shock* HENRY *and* EVELYN *just stand, motionless, looking at one another.*)
LAZAN	(*off*) Hello? Hello?
	(LAZAN *appears at one of the windows by the front door, he peers in.*)
	(*Seeing them and shouting through.*) Don't worry. It's not carol singers.
HENRY	And you are . . . ?
LAZAN	Sorry?
HENRY	Who-are-you?
LAZAN	Oh, right, of course. (LAZAN *fumbles in a coat pocket and brings out an ID card. He thrusts it against the window.*) Detective Chief Inspector Lazan. Metropolitan Police.
EVELYN	(*collapsing onto a chair*) Oh my God.
HENRY	(*steadying himself and shouting*) Good evening, Detective Chief Inspector. What can we do for you?
LAZAN	Well for a start, I'm a soft southerner and I'm freezing out here. Could you let me in?

HENRY	Er . . . yes. Of course. What am I thinking?
	(HENRY *goes to the front door and with one last meaningful look towards his wife, he lets* LAZAN *in.*)
LAZAN	Ah. Thank you. Good evening, sir.
HENRY	Good evening.
LAZAN	I'm sorry, I didn't catch your name.
HENRY	Henry Roth.
LAZAN	Mr Roth.
	(*They shake hands.*)
	(*Seeing* EVELYN.) Good evening, madam.
HENRY	And my wife, Evelyn.
LAZAN	Mrs Roth.
	(*She gets up and they shake hands. She winces slightly from her knife wound.*)
	Are you all right?
EVELYN	Yes, fine. Thank you. Just a sprain.
LAZAN	I see. Ah, how lovely . . .
	(LAZAN *goes and stands by the fireplace, warming himself for a moment.*)
HENRY	I'm sorry, it was DCI . . . ?
LAZAN	Lazan. Met Police.

HENRY: Lazan?

LAZAN: That's right. Londoner born and bred but of Croatian stock originally. Most people seem to think it's French.

HENRY: Uh huh. And what can we do for you this evening, Detective?

LAZAN: Probably something to do with it sounding like Lausanne.

HENRY: Which is in Switzerland.

LAZAN: Yes, quite right. But the French-speaking part.

HENRY: I wouldn't know. Never been.

LAZAN: No? Me neither. (*To* EVELYN.) Lovely house, by the way.

EVELYN: Thank you.

LAZAN: Victorian?

HENRY: Mid-Victorian. An ex-hunting lodge from the days when Victoria made the highlands very fashionable for holidaying.

LAZAN: Prefer the Algarve myself, but all my taste is in my mouth, as my wife would say. Yes, lovely place. Interesting décor. You see . . . Mrs Lazan would put a rug there.

(*He nods to where the rug was in Act One.*)

Ever thought about that? My wife, she's obsessed with rugs. I think it's an illness.

	Not that you need a rug you understand. Each to their own.
HENRY	Indeed. So, what is this . . .
LAZAN	. . . No decorations up yet? It's Christmas Eve tomorrow.
HENRY	We're well aware of that, thank you. We're just not in that festive a mood this year.
LAZAN	Oh dear, I'm sorry to hear that. A recent death?
EVELYN	What?
LAZAN	That's normally why people can't stand Christmas isn't it? The first Christmas after the death of a loved one.
HENRY	No, that's got nothing to do with it. We're just not . . . the Christmas type.
LAZAN	Oh. I see. How odd. I'm a fanatic myself. I even have a flashing sleigh and reindeer on my roof.
HENRY	How delightful.
LAZAN	The kids love it. Can't say the same for my neighbours but it's only once a year, isn't it?
HENRY	That's very true.
LAZAN	I suppose in my line of work you need a bit of light. A few festivities. God knows I spend the rest of the year buried up to my eyes in blood and murder. Does me good to have a few days of mulled wine, bad jokes

	and flashing sleighs. Shakes the bad stuff off, you know.
HENRY	I can imagine. Now, Detective, I think you owe it to me and my wife to tell us what a police officer from the Metropolitan Police is doing visiting a couple in the highlands of Scotland.
LAZAN	Oh, yes of course. I just assumed you would have guessed.
EVELYN	Guessed?
LAZAN	The Ghoul.
HENRY	The Ghoul? Oh . . . the murderer chap?
LAZAN	Yes, the murderer chap.
HENRY	Of course, is that still going on? Yes, that's right. You lot were brought in the assist the inept local bobbies.
LAZAN	Well, our PR department wouldn't put it quite like that but, yes. Broadly speaking. And I'm in charge, you see.
HENRY	So you haven't caught him yet?
LAZAN	No. Not yet. But we're closing in.
EVELYN	How can you be so sure?
LAZAN	I have a scent for these things.
HENRY	But surely you can't think that he's still around here. He's murdered people all over the country.

LAZAN	He has.
HENRY	Well, I know I'm not a detective, but even I would assume he would have moved on by now. The latest murder was where . . .
LAZAN	Glen Rellik.
HENRY	That's right. That's not far from here. Not by highland standards at least. You can't possibly think he's just hung around to be caught.
LAZAN	Ah, but you've just said it. 'Not by highland standards.'
HENRY	I'm sorry . . . ?
LAZAN	Well that's just it. Compared to the other locations of his murders, the highlands of Scotland are vast and far less inhabited. What's he going to do now? Head south? I doubt it. Leave the country? Impossible, the security is too high. So, we reckon he's going to be hiding up here, the most desolate spot in mainland Britain. It would make sense. A man can go missing in this landscape and not be found for years, if ever, if he so wished. With all your mountains and lakes, or is that lochs? Yes, very easy to just, disappear.
HENRY	I suppose it is. You've got a tough task on your hands, Detective.
LAZAN	I prefer it that way. Keeps me busy.
HENRY	And quite apart from that, you're chasing the invisible man, aren't you?

LAZAN	How do you mean?
HENRY	Well, from what I hear no one even knows what he looks like.
LAZAN	Ah, well, that was true until a couple of days ago. But you see we have far greater brains than mine working on this. Those clever chaps in Special Branch and in forensics got together and came up with a breakthrough.
HENRY	Really? Do tell.
LAZAN	The wounds of the victims were made by a very specific knife. A blade that is illegal in this country, even for hunting. After a lot of searching we found a knife with a blade that matches the wounds of the victims. It was for sale in a shady little shop in London. Peckham to be exact.
EVELYN	Peckham?
HENRY	Yes, Peckham, darling. It's in South London. Do keep up. Carry on, Detective.
LAZAN	Fearing for his livelihood, the owner of the shop told us that the knife was an illegal import and that he'd sold it to a young man a few weeks previously. He gave us a detailed description and we managed to get a pretty accurate photo fit of the suspect.
HENRY	Well . . . photo fits really aren't that useful, are they?
LAZAN	No, no you're right, Mr Roth. It pains me to say it, but you are. However, the other lot at Special Branch managed to source some

	CCTV footage from about a month ago of a young man getting on a train from Euston. The Fort William train, to be exact. I guess that must be the train you use whenever you head south.
HENRY	We very rarely head south.
LAZAN	No? Anyway, this footage landed on my desk and I in turn showed it to the shopkeeper and he confirmed it was the same young man who had bought the knife a few weeks earlier. From this photo we were able to find out who he was, where he's from and pretty much everything else about him. Now even you, Mr Roth, must be able to see that *that* is what we call a breakthrough.
HENRY	Yes. I suppose so.
LAZAN	Is everything all right, Mrs Roth?
EVELYN	I'm sorry? Yes, it's just a little disconcerting isn't it? A murderer travelling up here. On the same train that we catch. (*Beat.*) Tell me, this man. You know his name?
LAZAN	I do.
	(*Pause.* LAZAN *warms his hands on the fire again.*)
HENRY	Well . . . ?
LAZAN	Oh, I see. Sorry, Mr Roth. I've been so impressed with your observations thus far I thought I had a real life Miss Marple on my hands and that you were going to name him for me.

HENRY	And how would I do that, exactly?
LAZAN	Who knows?
EVELYN	His name, Detective . . .
LAZAN	Reed. Matthew Reed.

(HENRY *collapses into a chair and inadvertently laughs with relief.*)

	Something funny, Mr Roth?
HENRY	No, no I'm sorry. It's just you end up getting so worked up in situations like this that you persuade yourself you're going to know them.
LAZAN	And you don't?
HENRY	Matthew Reed? Never heard of him.
LAZAN	Mrs Roth?
EVELYN	No. Never met anyone by that name.
LAZAN	You've never met anyone by that name. Well, that's a start, I suppose.
HENRY	It would appear to me to be an end, if I may say so, Detective. We've never heard of him. Never met him. I think it's time you made your way to your next appointment. I'm sorry we can't help.
LAZAN	Perhaps. But you just said a very interesting thing.
HENRY	I do try.

LAZAN	'We have never heard of him. We have never met him.' They are two completely different things are they not?
HENRY	I don't see how.
LAZAN	Well, you may not have heard of Matthew Reed but you may easily have met him.
HENRY	If you're going to be that pedantic. I may have met many people, indeed I *have* met many people that I haven't heard of, doesn't mean we can help you catch this man.
LAZAN	True. But why don't we see if you have met him. Even if you don't know him.
HENRY	Fine, although I do think you could be spending your time more wisely, Detective.
	(LAZAN *takes a photo from a jacket pocket and places it on top of the coffee table. Takes a moment to notice the letters. He stands back.* HENRY *sighs, gets up to have a look. He stops dead. Picks it up. Inspects it more closely.*)
	No . . . no . . . still none the wiser I'm afraid. What do you think darling?
	(*He hands her the photograph. She struggles not to react.*)
LAZAN	Look very carefully please, Mrs Roth. This really is vitally important.
EVELYN	(*eventually getting words out*) No, I have no idea who this is. I'm terribly sorry.

	(*She quickly gets up and throws the photo back onto the coffee table.*)
LAZAN	I see. That's a shame. I hoped we would've had another breakthrough there. (*Long pause. Clapping his hands.*) Well! I've outstayed my welcome, I fear. Er . . . would you mind if I used your facilities before I go?
HENRY	What? Oh, of course. Up the stairs, door at the end of the corridor.
LAZAN	Much obliged. (LAZAN *makes his way up the stairs and exits.*)
EVELYN	(*making sure he's gone in hushed whisper*) Henry!
HENRY	Ssshhhh! Not until he's left the house.
EVELYN	It's him. It's Jack.
HENRY	I can see that.
EVELYN	Well what are we going to do?
HENRY	Absolutely nothing. If anything we've done him a favour. We've done the whole bloody nation a favour, we killed a serial killer! God, can you imagine . . . he was here. Actually here.
EVELYN	Should we tell him?
HENRY	Are you mad? Of course we shouldn't!
EVELYN	But he could stop the investigation. We could save him all that time, all that money.

HENRY	What a comforting thought to accompany us to our prison cells.
EVELYN	You still think we'd be charged with murder?
HENRY	Of course we would. They're hardly going pat us on the back and wish us all the best are they? No, no . . . we'll just let him leave then sit tight as the investigation blows over. Then we know we've got away with it.
EVELYN	You promised me we'd get away with it anyway.
HENRY	And we will. As long as we're not careless.
	(*A large bang from upstairs. They both jump.* LAZAN *enters from upstairs.*)
LAZAN	Sorry about that. It was freezing up there, a window was open in one of the bedrooms. I hope you don't mind but I shut it.
EVELYN	I thought you shut that window earlier?
HENRY	I did. I know I did.
LAZAN	Perhaps you've got a ghost.
EVELYN	What's that supposed to mean?
LAZAN	Nothing, sorry. Just an attempt at a joke. In bad taste I suppose with all this talk of murder.
	(*He places a hand on her arm. She winces from the pain from her wound and pulls away.*)

LAZAN	Carrying a war wound, Mrs Roth?
EVELYN	It's nothing.
HENRY	My wife fell a few days ago, it's just badly bruised.
LAZAN	Here, let me take a look.
EVELYN	No, honestly, it's fine.
LAZAN	Please, we have to do first aid in the force, I may be able to help.
HENRY	Honestly, it's nothing for you to worry about, Detective.
LAZAN	Nonsense, I've barged in and ruined your Christmas, I know I have, so please, let me take a look. (*Suddenly more serious.*) I won't go until I've had a look.
	(EVELYN *looks at* HENRY *and then slowly pulls her top down over her shoulder and shows the wound to* LAZAN.)
	You fell? On what exactly?
EVELYN	The . . . I can't quite . . .
HENRY	The radiator. Upstairs. You may have seen it. Surprisingly sharp edges.
LAZAN	I'd say.
	(EVELYN *pulls her top back up.*)
	I'd have that looked at if I were you. May even need stitches.

HENRY	Thank you, if it doesn't get better, we'll pop to the doctor after Christmas.
LAZAN	Do. And I'd look at changing your radiators. Right then. Oh, of course . . . can't forget that.

(LAZAN *goes to the coffee table and picks up the photograph. He starts to read the letters.*)

HENRY	Do you mind, they're private.
LAZAN	And quite threatening if I say so myself.
HENRY	Yes . . . well, it's nothing to worry about.
LAZAN	"You can't hide what you've done forever." "Someone knows of your crimes." "I'll see you soon. The truth will come to the surface."
HENRY	Thank you, Detective. They're just a practical joke sent by my agent.
LAZAN	A joke? Even worse than mine.
HENRY	Don't you worry, I'll tell him what I think all right. Please, it really isn't anything you should be concerning yourself with. You've enough to be getting on with.
LAZAN	I don't like the tone of these letters, Mr Roth. I can't help thinking that if it was a joke they'd be . . . funnier.
HENRY	Well, maybe it's not a joke. Maybe it's something I can't remember. I'm a successful man. I therefore have as many enemies as I have friends.

LAZAN   What is it you do, Mr Roth?

HENRY   I write plays. Thrillers to be exact.

LAZAN   Murder mysteries?

HENRY   Of sorts, yes.

LAZAN   How interesting.

HENRY   So you see, these could be from a number of people. A fan of my work even. Trying to feed me another plot. You know what they're like . . . fans.

LAZAN   I didn't know thriller writers had fans.

HENRY   Either way, these really aren't worth worrying about. In fact we were just about to burn them when you arrived.

LAZAN   I wouldn't do that. Just in case.

HENRY   In case of what?

LAZAN   In case they're real. Have you done many?

HENRY   Many what?

LAZAN   Crimes. It says here "someone knows of your crimes." What crimes would they be?

HENRY   Oh, I don't know. We've all done silly things haven't we? Even breaking the speed limit could be classed as a crime. It's rather easy to commit one when you think about it. So yes, probably. In the past, when I was a young man.

LAZAN	Seems odd to me that someone would be raking up something from your past, now. Of all times.
HENRY	(*going for the letters*) Well who knows, let's just leave it.
LAZAN	I'd rather not.
HENRY	(*eventually snatching them*) Well I'd rather you did!
LAZAN	There's no need to get so agitated.
HENRY	I think there is. You came here about something completely different, entirely. And now it seems as if you're suspecting me.
LAZAN	Of what?
HENRY	God knows, but that's what it seems like.
LAZAN	All I know, Mr Roth, is that someone is threatening you. And seemingly has enough over you to take the time to write you letters. I simply want to get to the bottom of that. In fact, I would say far from suspecting you, I'm actually trying to help you.
HENRY	Well it's not bloody helping is it?
	(*Pause.*)
LAZAN	Okay, Mr Roth. We'll leave it.
HENRY	Thank you.
LAZAN	For the time being. Maybe we'll come a nice full circle and end up right back here, with the letters.

HENRY I very much doubt it.

LAZAN Oh, I don't know. But as you say, these letters have nothing to do with why I came here in the first place. (*Beat.*) Unless of course they have something to do with The Ghoul.

EVELYN And why on earth would you think that?

LAZAN I don't 'think' anything, Mrs Roth. I am a detective. Everything I say comes from information that has been proved to be fact. Everything I do is done for a reason. Therefore, it is safe to assume I am here, in this house, talking to you, for a reason. Yes?

EVELYN And what is that reason?

LAZAN Suspicion, I suppose. I'm always suspicious of people who lie to me and you both have lied to me since I entered this house.

HENRY Lied about what, exactly?

LAZAN As you said, perhaps you didn't know Matthew Reed, but you certainly know the man in that photograph. A few background checks have shown that he has had a number of aliases since his teenage years but the one you both came in contact with was Jack Willoughby, an actor. Am I right? Don't just stare at me blankly, give me more credit than that. Firstly, Mr Roth. Playwright. We know from Reed's phone records that he spoke to you on the phone just over a month ago for nearly twenty minutes. You called, from this number. Here. We also know that you actually saw Jack Willoughby in a play at the Royal Court theatre in London. Not

	only do we have the ticket database from the theatre but we also have CCTV footage of you entering and leaving the theatre with another man, whom we later learned was Andrew Earl, your agent and the man you seem to want to blame these letters on. As for you, Mrs Roth, this is where the coincidences become all too neat for my liking. We have footage of you travelling to his flat in Peckham on the number 343 bus and this photograph (*He produces a photo from his jacket.*) of you and Jack Willoughby at a café on Dean Street, London. As you can see, you are being rather cosy over your cappuccinos.
EVELYN	Where the hell did you get that?
LAZAN	So, by the looks on your faces I can only assume this isn't the first time Mrs Roth's adultery has been brought up in this household. What was it, some sort of bizarre theatrical love triangle?
HENRY	Don't be so crude. Yes, we know all this. It's a rather unsubtle way of dragging up ugly memories but it's true. I met Jack, or Matthew, at the Royal Court. My wife, quite independently, met him at some café near the theatre and they began an affair that lasted a number of months. We're not going to deny it. But not only are the two circumstances unconnected except for those involved but they have nothing to do with him being a murderer. I don't see what we've got to do with that part of the story.
LAZAN	Because I'm looking for him and you both know where he is. (*Pause.*) Oh come on! We know he caught a train up here a month ago. We know he committed a murder in

| | Glen Rellik only twenty miles from here that same day. Are you telling me he didn't come here? Didn't come to hide out with two people whom he knew and who would, on seeing him, welcome him into their house and give him shelter and at the same time a cover story? |

HENRY   That's really not how it was.

LAZAN   So he was here.

(HENRY *and* EVELYN *look at one another.*)

HENRY   Fine. Yes he was here.

EVELYN Henry . . .

HENRY   But he was here as Jack Willoughby, the actor. And it was all my doing.

LAZAN   Explain.

HENRY   I brought him in under the pretence of seeing him for a part in my next play. Yes, I had spoken to him on the phone. Told him some cock and bull story about being in awe of his acting talent and that I wanted him for the lead role in my next production. The truth was that I had uncovered his seedy little affair with my wife and I wanted to call him out on it. I wanted to see the looks on both their faces when I let them know it was no longer a secret.

LAZAN   And you knew about this, Mrs Roth?

EVELYN No. I mean, Henry told me he'd invited someone to the house but exactly who, I

	wasn't sure. Not until I came into the room did I know it was Jack.
HENRY	That's true, Detective. I wanted it to be a surprise.
LAZAN	A slightly twisted and long-winded way of going about things, don't you think?
HENRY	Perhaps. But they'd had their fun, I wanted mine.
LAZAN	And what happened?
HENRY	Well, what do you expect?
LAZAN	I'd expect you to have killed him. (*Beat.*) Well . . . ?
HENRY	I did exactly as I have said. I confronted them with my knowledge of their affair. Told them how angry I was, how upset. (*He looks at his wife.*) But then, we talked. Just talked. I said that if they really loved one another they could have each other. I wasn't going to support them or be pleased for them but if that's they wanted they could leave. Together.
LAZAN	Really? That's what you said?
HENRY	That's what I said. Evelyn?
EVELYN	Yes . . . That's what happened.
LAZAN	Yet I assume your presence here suggests you didn't take up the offer.

HENRY
: No, Detective. My wife saw sense. Apologised and asked for forgiveness. Which I duly gave. She chose me.

LAZAN
: And Jack, he just took this on the chin did he and left?

HENRY
: He was upset, of course. But he soon realised he had no chance of changing my wife's mind and yes, he left. We assume to go back to London.

LAZAN
: I see. How wonderfully tidy.

HENRY
: Perhaps, but it's the truth.

LAZAN
: You really expect me to believe that an unhinged sociopath simply shrugged his shoulders and left to go home.

HENRY
: I didn't know he was an unhinged sociopath, if I did do you really think I would have invited him here? So yes, Detective. He simply left to go home. And that's all we can tell you.

LAZAN
: So what would you say if I told you he didn't go home? In fact he didn't even leave the area as far as we can tell.

HENRY
: I don't know what we'd say except that it's not our responsibility. He left our home. He left our lives. We've told you the truth, Detective. We can't help you any more.

LAZAN
: Fine. So I'm just going to take your word that you're not harbouring a known murderer.

EVELYN
: Harbouring? You must be joking.

HENRY	We haven't seen him since. He could be in Timbuktu for all we know.
LAZAN	So how about this for a news bulletin? Yours truly identified, chased and subsequently lost the murderer in town, not twenty minutes from here, whilst patrolling the Christmas festival.
HENRY	That's impossible.
LAZAN	And why's that?
HENRY	The Christmas festival only opened yesterday.
LAZAN	I know. He was spotted this afternoon.

(*Silence.*)

EVELYN	Are you . . . absolutely certain?
LAZAN	Of course.
HENRY	Darling . . . ?
LAZAN	Mrs Roth? Is everything all right?
EVELYN	No, Detective! Everything is not all right.
HENRY	Evelyn, calm down. There's a simple explanation.
EVELYN	Really, Henry? Go on then . . . give me that simple explanation. Go on . . . explain this!
LAZAN	What on earth is the matter? If either of you know anything, you have got to tell me, do you understand? Mrs Roth?

EVELYN	Detective . . .
HENRY	Evelyn, you can't . . .
EVELYN	Oh shut up, Henry! Shut up! You know as well as I do we have to tell him. I knew as soon as he walked into the house we were going to have to come clean eventually.
LAZAN	Come clean?
HENRY	My wife is hysterical, Detective . . . I'm sorry about this.
EVELYN	I am not hysterical. It all makes sense now. Seeing him, feeling his eyes on me. God . . . And you never believed me.
HENRY	Well of course I didn't. He's dead!
LAZAN	I'm sorry?
EVELYN	Detective, I killed him. I killed Matthew Reed.
LAZAN	That's impossible.
EVELYN	Or at least I thought I had. This wound, you knew it wasn't from a fall. It was a knife. His knife. He attacked me, after we'd asked him to leave, he lost it, turned on me and was going to kill me. But I managed to break free and . . . I killed him. Stabbed him to be precise.
LAZAN	So where's the body?
EVELYN	I tied the body up in a rug, weighed it down with stones gathered from the shore, rowed

	into the loch and dropped his body over the side.
LAZAN	And you can verify this, Mr Roth?
HENRY	Well . . . you see Detective, I had gone to bed. I learned about it in the morning.
LAZAN	You didn't assist your wife in the killing or with the disposing of the body?
HENRY	No.
	(HENRY *avoids* EVELYN's *disbelieving stare*.)
LAZAN	Well, I'm afraid, somewhere along the line you made a mistake . . . because he is not at the bottom of a loch, I can assure you.
EVELYN	I know that now. I should have made sure, but I panicked in the boat.
LAZAN	How do you mean?
EVELYN	As I rowed out, I was getting ready to push his body overboard. I could barely lift him, so I used an oar as a lever. I stuck it under his body and against the seat in the boat and pushed down. The body . . . oh, God . . . it was horrible! This dead weight slowly lifted into the air and just before it was about to fall over the edge . . . (*She can barely continue*.)
LAZAN	What? Mrs Roth, what happened?
EVELYN	His arm came shooting out of the top of the rug . . .
HENRY	Good God.

EVELYN	It was horrible, like something from a horror movie. I panicked. I didn't know what to do so I just pushed down harder on the oar. The body went over the side and I rowed back, as fast as I could.
LAZAN	Did you see the body sink? (*Beat.*) Mrs Roth . . . did you actually watch the body sink?
EVELYN	No! It was too dark and I was too scared.
HENRY	You can't possibly think that he escaped.
LAZAN	You can't take anything for granted with this man. I've seen him in the area. By all accounts so has your wife.
EVELYN	I . . . I couldn't be sure . . . I thought it was a dream . . .
LAZAN	I fear it was very much reality. He's playing with you. With you both. He hasn't left the area for a reason. And I now know that reason is you. Your lives are in danger. He knows who I am. He'll no doubt have been watching the house and has seen me arrive. That window, the one upstairs. You said you'd shut it earlier.
HENRY	I'm pretty sure I had . . .
EVELYN	You don't think he's here? Now?
LAZAN	I do. (LAZAN *takes out a mobile phone.*)
EVELYN	What are you doing?
LAZAN	I'm calling for backup. My squad is based in the town. No signal. (*He goes to the*

landline. Picks up the phone, then replaces the receiver very slowly.)

HENRY   What's wrong?

LAZAN   The phone line's dead.

EVELYN   It's him, isn't it? Oh God, he's here!

LAZAN   Calm down, Mrs Roth. I need you both to calm down.

(*A bang from an upstairs door.* LAZAN *takes out a handgun from a holster we haven't yet seen.*)

HENRY   Is that really necessary?

(LAZAN *makes his way to the foot of the stairs.*)

EVELYN   This is a nightmare . . . this must be a nightmare . . .

LAZAN   Shhh!

(LAZAN *makes his way up the stairs, stopping before he leaves view. Silence. A figure walks past the windows, unseen.*)

          Mr Roth, tell me how many entrances and exits are there to the house.

HENRY   Well, apart from the front door, of course, there's the old servant's entrance into the kitchen. And there's the garden room from the library.

LAZAN   Too many for my liking.

(A heavy bang on the window by the desk. They all spin around, startled.)

LAZAN I want you both to stay here. Don't move from this room. Do you understand? Lock the door behind me.

(LAZAN makes his way carefully out of the front door, we see him pass the window out of sight. EVELYN locks the door before heading towards the kitchen.)

HENRY Where are you going?

EVELYN I need something . . . anything to stop me feeling like a sitting duck. *(She exits into kitchen.)*

HENRY Evelyn! Don't . . .

(Pause. The library door starts to move. HENRY backs away, slowly towards the kitchen door.)

HENRY Please . . . oh my God . . .

(He's almost at the kitchen door when EVELYN comes out at pace holding a carving knife. The library door slams shut. They make each other scream.)

You almost killed me! What the hell's that for?

EVELYN For you.

HENRY What am I meant to do with that?

EVELYN Be a man for once! Protect your wife.

	(HENRY *reluctantly takes the knife, holds it awkwardly.*)
HENRY	Where the hell is Lazan?
	(*The figure appears at the window again unseen, looks in.* EVELYN *senses something, turns around but he's moved beyond the far window and out of sight. Pause. "Carols from King's" starts to play from the library.*)
EVELYN	Henry?
HENRY	Shhh!
	(HENRY *slowly approaches the library door.*)
	Lazan? Detective Lazan, is that you?
	(*The lights go out. Carols stop playing.*)
EVELYN	Henry, what's going on?
HENRY	He's here.
	(*Suddenly a figure bursts through the library door,* HENRY *roars and* EVELYN *screams.* HENRY *plunges the knife into the figure who collapses onto* HENRY. *As the figure staggers into the room, the lights come back on. It's* LAZAN. *He has blood on his hands from the wound that he clutches.*)
	Oh God, no! Detective . . . !
	(HENRY *rushes to him and tries to hold him up, but his weight is too much and he slips through his arms,* HENRY *now has blood on his hands, he clasps these hands round* LAZAN'S *face.*)

HENRY	Detective, I didn't know . . . I thought . . .
LAZAN	(*struggling to speak*) This wasn't . . . meant . . . to . . .

(*He collapses, behind the settee, almost out of sight. Dead.* HENRY *drops the knife, he is in shock.*)

EVELYN   Henry? Henry it was an accident. For God's sake, Henry!

(EVELYN *speedily takes* LAZAN'S *gun.*)

Fine. You stay here if you want but I'm not going to just wait around to be killed.

(*As she says the above* EVELYN *unlocks the front door, opens it and turns around to speak to* HENRY *without looking out. We see the figure, who is of course* JACK, *standing there, a look of hatred on his face. Leather gloves on, knife in hand. She turns back to exit . . .*)

HENRY   Evelyn!

(*She turns into* JACK *who plunges a knife into her, deeper and deeper. Blood is seen. He discards her body, dumping it onto a window seat before she flops onto the floor.*)

No! Please . . .

(HENRY *rushes to the body but* JACK *stops him.*)

JACK   Don't! Stay exactly where you are. (JACK *retrieves the gun from* EVELYN'S *hand.*) I'm not a fan of such crude instruments. They lack any sense of art. (*He casually points the gun at* HENRY.) Still, they do help to make sure someone doesn't make a run for it. Though I don't think I'll have that trouble with you, will I Hopalong Cassidy? Now sit down.

(HENRY *does so.*)

HENRY How . . . how is this happening?

JACK Never heard of someone coming back from the dead? Let's call it, the Rasputin effect, shall we? You know Rasputin was poisoned with cyanide and shot six times before his murderers decided he was dead. Then they threw his body into the frozen river and still, the next day, there were scratch marks on the ice where he had tried to drag himself out of the frozen water with his fingers. Now that's impressive. Compared to that my escape is really rather tame.

HENRY You're him. You're the Ghoul.

JACK A silly nickname. An attempt to make me a monster when in fact I'm just an extraordinary human being. (*He starts to laugh . . .*) But you know what's funny? Barely a month ago, we were in this room and you were asking me to 'get into the mind of a psychopath'! You didn't know how easy that was for me.

HENRY And now you're going to kill me. Please, I beg you . . . just do it, please don't . . . just get it over with.

JACK No, no. Let's not get carried away. I don't kill men. (*Nodding towards* LAZAN.) You

evidently do, but that's your bag. I only
kill women. It's a little quirk of mine. Now,
you wanted to get inside the head of a
psychopath, I'll let you inside mine. I have
no interest in killing you. I will if needs be,
but I won't enjoy it. But I do have an interest
in people keeping their promises. That's
why I came back. To fulfil my promise. Now
you've got to fulfil yours.

HENRY I don't understand.

JACK Bloody hell, Henry. Is the old memory going
as well as the eyesight? You asked me to kill
your wife for a rather large sum of money.
I've done that now. So . . .

HENRY You want me to pay you?

JACK Ta dah! We have put two and two together.
Of course I do. I need the money. I can't
go back to London. I need to shed my skin
again. I've done it before. I was Matthew
Reed for long enough, now Jack Willoughby
has to go. So . . . the money, please.

HENRY But . . . I can't. The police will know I've
transferred the money. I'll be an accessory
to murder.

JACK What happens to you is your concern.
We made a deal. Only a click of a button
remember, and it's done. Now!

(HENRY *eases himself up and under the
watchful gaze of* JACK *makes his way to the
laptop and sits down.*)

HENRY Give me a minute.

JACK	The amount we agreed on.
HENRY	Of course.

(JACK *turns away to look out of the window, he's edgy.*)

HENRY	And I'll need . . .

(HENRY *spots the bank card from* EVELYN'S *account on the desk.*)

JACK	What?
HENRY	Nothing.
JACK	You've still got my account details I hope.
HENRY	Yes . . . I kept your card, here.
JACK	Go on then, I haven't got all night.

(JACK *goes back to the window.* HENRY *keys in some details for a moment and then some numbers. He presses 'Enter'.*)

Okay, it's done.

(JACK *marches over to the computer and looks over* HENRY'S *shoulder. He puts the gun down on the desk.*)

JACK	What am I looking at?
HENRY	(*nervous, hoping this is going to work*) There, that's the amount transferred. It's just gone through.

(*Beat.*)

JACK	See. Almost as easy as murder.
	(JACK *snatches the bank card from* HENRY'S *hand a slips it into a pocket.*)
	But then, it's the getting away with it that's the trick.
HENRY	Very true.
	(JACK *goes to the front door leaving the gun on the desk. He opens the door and turns around.*)
JACK	Looks to me like you have some tidying up to do. Well . . . I'm sure you'll just blame it all on me. I would. Goodbye, Henry. (*He turns to leave, then stops dead. Turns back slowly and enters the room again. He's spotted something on the floor.*)
HENRY	What is it?
	(JACK *goes to the side of the settee, bends down, reaches underneath and pulls out a bank card. This is* JACK'S *from Act One.*)
JACK	What's this?
HENRY	I . . . I don't know.
JACK	This is my bank card. The one I gave you a month ago. How did it end up here?
HENRY	It must have . . .
JACK	And more importantly, whose is this? (*He takes out the other bank card and reads.*) 'Mrs Evelyn Roth'. This is your wife's account. You've just paid my money into

	your dead wife's account! (*He throws the card at him.*)
HENRY	Like I said . . . the police will notice if I pay you! They'll be watching your account. Look, I'll give you a cheque.
JACK	(*approaching* HENRY *with his knife held aloft*) I don't like weak people who don't fulfil their promises!
HENRY	No, please. I will pay . . . I will, give me your card.
JACK	Too late, Henry, too bloody late.

(*He goes for* HENRY, *but* HENRY *swipes him with his cane, hits him on the head and has the time to grab the gun, turn around and shoot* JACK. JACK *staggers, holding his chest. He tries to walk towards* HENRY *but rests on the edge of the settee, then the death throes slowly become more and more elaborate until they become ridiculous. He seemingly dies and then opens his eyes . . .*)

And that's what you call Royal Court acting! (*He gets up and takes a bow.*) Thank you. Thank you. Too kind. And may I introduce my partner without whom none of this would be possible, Mrs Evelyn Roth.

(EVELYN *gets up.* JACK *applauds her.*)

JACK	Bravo! Bravo! Splendid!
EVELYN	Thank you, Jack. That's enough.
JACK	Oh come on! Even you must be surprised it's gone so well.

EVELYN	Surprised? Hardly. It was planned meticulously. And dear Henry. As predictable as one of your plays.
HENRY	What . . . what's going on? Is this some sick joke?
EVELYN	Exactly. As sick as the joke you played on me my entire married life with you.
HENRY	But you were stabbed . . . by him . . .
EVELYN	Blood capsules, Henry. Just like when I plunged the knife into Jack a month ago.
JACK	And blanks in the gun. As a thriller writer you of all people should know how useful they can be.
EVELYN	In fact, very little that has happened in the last few months is as it seems. Except for the essentials. Yes, Jack and I met in London and yes, we fell in love. But far from trying to hide it from you, we planned from the outset that you should find out. Fully aware that you were checking up on me at the clinic and aware that you followed me, we allowed you to play your little game. And we played ours. If you hadn't come up with the idea of paying Jack to kill me, he'd have put the idea into your head. We knew you'd go for it. And the thriller was on. Planned to the final curtain. The twist, however, and with thrillers it always comes down to the twist, was how to make sure we had something over you. Like you had over me.
HENRY	What do you mean?

EVELYN	You trapped me and refused to let me live my own life. Punishing me for a mistake I made all those years ago.
JACK	And when it seemed she had finally found happiness, instead of accepting it as an inevitability you conspired to have her murdered . . . a crime you didn't even have the guts to commit yourself, instead paying someone else to do it with the money you never let your wife have.
EVELYN	If that's not a sick joke, I don't know what is.
HENRY	And do you really think I'm going to let you get away with this?
EVELYN	Yes, because you have to. We're the only two witnesses to your murder.
HENRY	Murder . . . you mean, Lazan? He's really . . .
JACK	Yes. He really is. But I'm sure you've guessed by now, he wasn't really DCI Lazan. He was my flatmate, Matthew Reed.
HENRY	. . . But why?
JACK	It's a thriller, Henry! Someone's got to die.
EVELYN	And we needed to make sure you'd keep paying the money you owe me.
JACK	(*having picked up the bank card and waving it between his fingers*) Thanks for the first instalment, by the way. I bet you thought you'd tricked me back there. Make it look as if you'd paid money into my account when in fact you'd paid it into your dead wife's.

	Meaning of course, it was as good as yours. Clever. If she was dead, that is.
EVELYN	It's a shame, but Matthew was the lamb to the slaughter. An innocent loner who no one, except perhaps his dopey girlfriend, will really miss.
HENRY	You're mad.
EVELYN	That's your fault. You drove me to it, made me mad with desperation.
HENRY	Okay. I killed him. But the police will realise . . . I had no reason to. You may say this is a thriller and there has to be a victim, but there has to be a motive too. And I don't have that.
JACK	Ah, but you do. You've just murdered your blackmailer.
HENRY	I'm sorry?
JACK	I told you a month ago, Matthew here went away most weekends so Evelyn and I could easily use his computer to compose rather vague but threatening blackmail letters. We saved them to his computer and printed them off. That computer is now in our possession.
EVELYN	Jack then gave him the letters to post. He did some temp work for a firm of architects. Jack asked him if he could use the franking machine at work and save him precious money on stamps. As they were addressed to Halliwell & Partner they looked genuine enough and the office manager simply

	posted them off. He did this once a week for the last month.
JACK	So as for evidence of your motive, we're swimming in it. All the police and a jury will see is that Matthew Reed had something over you and was threatening you with letters he posted from his place of work.
EVELYN	One letter even states that he will 'see you soon' . . . so alongside his rail tickets, there's the evidence of his being here.

(JACK *goes over to* LAZAN's *body and picks up the knife.*)

JACK	And, not forgetting there's a knife here with the victim's blood and your fingerprints all over it. (JACK *takes out a clear, plastic bag and drops the knife in.*) The essential props of a murderer, don't you agree, Henry?
EVELYN	So, all you need to do is keep those details of that bank account you kindly opened for me and pay in enough money every month so we can enjoy our life together. But if even one month is missed, we assure you there'll be a laptop and a murder weapon anonymously sent to the detective in charge of finding Matthew Reed.
HENRY	But . . . he was Lazan?
JACK	Henry, he's an out of work actor itching for any role he can get his hands on. It was easy to promise him a share of the spoils and get him here. We even directed him, told him how to play it, let him in on the entire back story.

EVELYN	We left nothing to chance, told him to draw attention to the letters, told him to quiz me on the carefully choreographed wound on my arm and gave him a gun filled with blanks.
HENRY	But he was here looking for the Ghoul . . . that can't just be coincidence?
EVELYN	Of course it's not. Because it's not even true. You made the error that your audience makes . . . taking people's word for things. Who read you the original article about the Ghoul? Me. I made it up. Making sure I dropped the name Detective Chief Inspector Lazan into the mix. Check the newspaper, it's not in there.

(HENRY *rushes over to the newspapers by the fireplace and starts fumbling through them manically.*)

JACK	Who told you the Ghoul was spotted in town today?
EVELYN	Matthew, because we told him to.
JACK	Who told you the phone was dead?
EVELYN	You see . . . all carefully planned.
JACK	We couldn't have you thinking the phone actually worked. That's the death of any thriller.

(HENRY *stops looking, slumped by the fireplace in a pile of discarded newspaper.*)

HENRY	How did you know? How could you be certain I'd kill him?

JACK	We had to rely on . . . how would you put it? 'The piquancy of the moment'. Spend enough time working someone up so that they're in fear for their own life and they're ready to kill.
EVELYN	The last month dropping hints here and there, just enough for you to doubt whether Jack's body was in fact at the bottom of that loch.
JACK	You weren't to know I got out of the rowing boat long before you saw Evelyn dump something over the side. At night, from shore . . . you just *assumed* it was my body.
EVELYN	And your eyes really aren't what they used to be.
JACK	So tonight I just had to tell Matthew when to make his grand entrance. As soon as I knew you were coiled tight as a spring. But you would know all about that. With thrillers, it's all about timing.
HENRY	But you could have just pretended to kill Evelyn a month ago, like you pretended to kill Jack. You would still have got your money.
EVELYN	True, but it would only have been a one off payment. We reckon you owe me more than that. Oh, come on, Henry! Don't look so glum. You should be proud. All these tricks, all the twists, lies and hoodwinks. I learned them all from you. (EVELYN *goes to the drawer and takes out the car keys.*) I do hope this next play is as *seismic* as you think. You need the money. Goodbye, husband dear. Don't forget me. (*She bends*

down to look him in the eyes.) You can't afford to.

JACK I would tell you what to do with the body, but I think you already know. Hope you've got another rug. See you around, Henry.

(EVELYN *and* JACK *exit the front door, shutting it behind them.* HENRY *eventually staggers to his feet. We hear the car pull away.*

HENRY *looks at* LAZAN'S *body for a moment. Then he goes and sits in the centre of the settee, head in hands. The clock marks the hour: 6 p.m. As the clock falls silent,* HENRY *raises his head from his hands and looks straight out to the audience.*

Silence.

Suddenly, the bloodied arm of LAZAN *appears threateningly over the back of the settee . . . about to grab* HENRY *. . .*

Cut to blackout. The end.)